NORTHUMBERLAND COUNTY, VIRGINIA

REGISTERS OF FREE BLACKS

by

Karen E. Sutton, MA

HERITAGE BOOKS
2016

HERITAGE BOOKS
AN IMPRINT OF HERITAGE BOOKS, INC.

Books, CDs, and more—Worldwide

For our listing of thousands of titles see our website
at
www.HeritageBooks.com

Published 2016 by
HERITAGE BOOKS, INC.
Publishing Division
5810 Ruatan Street
Berwyn Heights, Md. 20740

International Standard Book Numbers
Paperbound: 978-0-7884-1132-8
Clothbound: 978-0-7884-6406-5

This book is dedicated to my ancestors and to those named herein.

May you never be forgotten.

TABLE OF CONTENTS

PREFACE

Traditionally we have seen the antebellum population of the United States in simple regional complexion terms. That is, Northerner or Southerner, and White or Black. However, there was a fifth category, which is just now beginning to be studied in depth. The fifth category contained a people who crossed the lines of the other four. By name they were the so-called "Free Blacks."

Whites categorized "nonwhite, non Asian people who were not enslaved for life as 'free colored.' Often these people were free born of free parents, had never known formal bondage (slavery), and often owed their status to the fact that their mothers were white.[1] However, they were not truly free in the sense that whites who were not indentured servants were free. An ever increasing series of restrictive laws governed so-called Free Blacks. Whites designed these laws especially for members of the darker race not controlled by the "Peculiar Institution."

I learned about the existence of the *Northumberland County Register* many years ago from the Director of the National Society *Daughters of the American Revolution* (DAR) Library in Washington, D.C. At the time she was researching Amos Nickens II, a Northumberland Free Black Seaman who served in the Virginia State Navy during the Revolutionary War. Mr. Eric Grundset, the Director, advised there was a list of Free Blacks before emancipation at the Courthouse in Heathsville. When she asked at the Courthouse, the clerks referred her to the local Historical Society. A member of the staff at the Northumberland Historical Society told her there were two lists. Each being named the "Register of Free Blacks." The first list covered the period 1803 to 1849. The second list continued with 1849 to 1858. This author requested a copy of the entire list (which is in the public domain and which she had to pay money for) The reply she received was *"You don't need all that. Just tell me what surnames you're working on, and I'll send those pages."* Again, the author still had to pay for the copies, and that information is in the public domain. The individual in question went on to say *"I gave the whole thing to Jimmy Walker when he spoke in Richmond. You don't need that."* This author knew the late Mr. Walker personally,[2] and when she questioned him about it, Mr. Walker admitted to having no idea where the document was, and added that he was not doing Virginia research. Not until 1996 was this author able to obtain a complete copy of both registers. She included an edited version of the registers as the final appendix in her Master's Project Paper, published in 1997. This is just one example of the obstacles encountered by African American researchers. Thank you to all those individuals who have not, do not, and will not be obstacles to the research of others.

---

[1]Sherrie S. McLeRoy, and William R. McLeRoy, *STRANGERS IN THEIR MIDST: The Free Black Population of Amehurst County, Virginia* (Bowie, MD: Heritage Books, Inc., 1993), p. 1.

[2]"Genealogist, James D. Walker, Dies at Age 65," *The Washington Post* 8 October 1993. The late Mr. Walker was one of the most well-known African American genealogists in white circles. He helped found *The Afro-American Historical & Genealogical Society.* This author once served as membership chairperson for that organization.

For many years, historians believed the first Africans in British North America landed near *Jamestown, Virginia* in August 1619. They were Antoney, Isabella, and Pedro, along with seventeen other Africans.[3] These "twenty and odd" Africans were the surviving cargo of more than one hundred Negroes aboard a Dutch man-of-war. The Dutch pilfered them from a Spanish frigate bound for the Spanish West Indies. The exact location of their landing is unknown, however, historical evidence suggests this event occurred at *Point Comfort*, the first port of call on the *James River*. Today, we call it *Old Point Comfort*, and it is at *Ft. Monroe*, a military installation south of the city of *Hampton, Virginia*.[4]

Now we know that before the seventeenth century, Africans first came to America as free men, and then from Europe with the Spanish and Portuguese as their "Ethiopian" servants. These early African emigrants may have already been mixed bloods, what Dr. Berlin calls "Atlantic Creoles," the offspring of relations between Europeans and Africans in the towns that emerged surrounding the slave castles on the west coast of Africa.[5] Because they were a hybrid group, neither the whites, nor the blacks fully accepted them. So, they were forced to form their own communities. When given the opportunity to travel, or when they were forced to do so (due to the transatlantic slave trade), these "Atlantic Creoles" merely transferred skills they learned in their native land to a new location.

---

[3]Lerone Bennett, Jr., *Before the Mayflower A History of Black America* (Chicago: Johnson Publishing Company, 1962; 6th rev. ed., New York: Penguin Books, 1993), pp. 29, 36, 45, 443; Workers of the Writers' Program of the Works Projects Administration in the State of Virginia, comp., *The Negro in Virginia* (New York: Hastings House, 1940; reprint Winston-Salem: John F. Blair, Publisher, 1994), pp. 1-2.

[4]Ibid; Robert Beverley, *The History and Present State of Virginia*, ed. Louis B. Wright (Chapel Hill: University of North Carolina Press, 1947), pp. 48, 349.

[5]Ira Berlin, "From Creole to African: Atlantic Creoles and the Origins of African-American Society in Mainland North America," *The William and Mary Quarterly* Third Series, LIII (April 1996): p. 254, note 8.

"Atlantic creole,' employed herein, designates those who by experience or choice, as well as by birth, became part of a new culture that emerged along the Atlantic littoral -- in Africa, Europe, or the Americas -- beginning in the 16th century. It departs from the notion of "creole" that makes birth definitive . . . Circumstances and volition blurred differences between "African" and "creole" as defined only by nativity, if only because Africans and creoles were connected by ties of kinship and friendship. They worked together, played together, intermarried, and on occasion stood together against assaults on their freedom. Even more important men and women could define themselves in ways that transcended nativity. 'African' and 'creole' were as much a matter of choice as of birth. The term 'Atlantic creole' is designed to capture the cultural transformation that sometimes preceded generational change and sometimes was unaffected by it."

According to William Thornedale, "The famous 20-plus Africans who came in August 1619 were not the first blacks to arrive. The census of early 1619 counts 32 Negroes already in the colony."[6] These Africans became indentured servants like many Europeans. Slavery did not become law in Virginia until 1661, but Virginia was not the first to legalize slavery. That dubious distinction belongs to the Massachusetts colony, whose residents recognized slavery in the law twenty years earlier in December 1641. Therefore, the first Africans in the British North American colonies were probably indentured servants. Many of these Africans, and those who followed them, worked out their indentures and became free, at least until the laws covering slavery hardened in 1705.

How did we come to this? The route to that decision was less direct than many have imagined. The process of black African disenfranchisement, and degradation was not orderly and planned. Parts of it were a response to life events. English and African landowners lived together as relative equals for almost a century. Bacon's Rebellion became the pivotal event in the downfall of black-white relations. The year was 1676. Fear was the reaction to Bacon's Rebellion, and the result was the slave codes of 1705. These codes hammered the final nail in the coffin of the truly free African in the American colonies.[7]

Nonslave Blacks.

The Slave Law of 1705 was legislation that created a new class -- the nonslave blacks.[8] Although there were a few free blacks before this, as a group, they were not large enough in numbers to form a class unto themselves. Because the black category on the Northumberland County Personal Property Tax Lists was for enslaved persons, and there was no category for free blacks, the tax collectors treated many of them as honorary whites.[9] They were a people exploited, a class whom whites tried to eliminate from their culture. Freedom for nonslave blacks was desperately insecure. It meant living on the edge. For them, the key to maintaining any dignity, or semblance of a free lifestyle was to own property. Colonial Virginia society revolved around ownership of the land. Members of the House of Burgesses, the law makers of colonial

---

[6]Peter H. Wood, "'I Did the Best I Could Do For My Day': The Study of Early Black History During the Second Reconstruction, 1960 to 1976," William and Mary Quarterly 35 (April 1976): pp. 185-186; William Thornedale, "The Virginia Census of 1619," Magazine of Virginia Genealogy 33 (Summer 1995): p. 155.

[7]T. H. Breen and Stephen Innes, "Myne Owne Ground:" Race and Freedom on Virginia's Eastern Shore, 1640-1676 (New York: Oxford University Press, 1980), pp. 4-6.

[8]European Americans labeled them free blacks or free persons of color.

[9]There was no category in Northumberland County's Personal Property Tax Lists for Free Blacks. The Black columns were for slaves. Free Blacks were enumerated with the white population.

Virginia, were all wealthy land owners. White men who did not own property could not vote.[10] What do we know about African Americans in the Virginia county studied here? Probably only a few people were considered as free blacks in Northumberland County, during the early colonial period.[11]

By the early eighteenth century, the free black class became less and less free according to law. The Burgesses systematically eliminated equality for blacks.[12] White law makers (Burgesses) brought the legal ability of blacks to interact equally with whites to a complete halt. These Burgesses also made it more difficult for owners to manumit enslaved persons. Before 1705, free blacks had the opportunity to aspire to the same lifestyle as whites. After 1705, for the most part, the growth of the free black community became limited to natural increase, or interaction with the few remaining Native Americans.[13] Other events which affected the number of free blacks were the 1723 law, the American Revolution, the 1782 law, and the 1783 law. Simultaneously, black African enslaved persons became the predominant labor force in America. The new slave society did not welcome free blacks. It just tolerated them.

Generally, free blacks comprised only a small part of any Virginia county's African American population.[14] By the time of the first federal census in 1790 (1782 to 1785 in Virginia), Virginia's total population was 747,610 persons. Of these, 442,117 or 59.14% were considered white. Of the nonwhite population 12,866 were categorized as free persons of color, and 292,627 were listed as enslaved persons. Statistically, non-whites comprised only 1.72% of the state population, whereas 39.14% of the state population were enslaved persons. (See Table 2) Berkeley County had the largest population overall with 19,713 persons, and Randolph County was the least populated with 951 occupants. Harrison, Randolph, and Rockingham Counties claimed no non-white free persons. Accomack County had the largest number of free persons

---

[10]Breen, *Myne Owne Ground*, pp. 4-6. Only white male property owners could vote. Women, nonslave blacks, mulattoes, and Indians were denied the vote, regardless of social position or income level.

[11]Often "black" did not mean Negro, it was a catchall term for anyone not clearly Caucasian.

[12]The colonial Virginia legislature was called the House of Burgesses. Individual members of the House were referred to as "burgesses."

[13]A few whites risked fine and punishment by becoming involved in serious relations with blacks.

[14]Douglas Deal, "A Constricted World Free Blacks on Virginia's Eastern Shore, 1680-1750," in *Colonial Chesapeake Society*, ed. Lois Green Carr, Philip D. Morgan, and Jean B. Russo (Chapel Hill: The University of North Carolina Press, 1988), pp. 276-277, 303-305; Philip D. Morgan, "Slave Life in Piedmont Virginia, 1720-1800," in *Colonial Chesapeake Society*, ed. Lois Green Carr, Philip D. Morgan, and Jean B. Russo (Chapel Hill: The University of North Carolina Press, 1988), p. 462.

of color. The largest number of enslaved persons resided in Amelia County, and the smallest number lived in Randolph County.[15] (See Table 1.)

Table 1. Race and Status Breakdown of the 1790 Census for Selected Virginia Counties in Comparison with Northumberland County.[16]

| Name of County | Number of Whites | | Number of Nonwhites | | | | Total Population |
| | | | Free | | Enslaved persons | | |
	No.	% of Total	No.	% of Total	No.	% of Total	
Accomack	8,976	64.30%	721	5.17%	4,262	30.53%	13,959
Amelia[17]	6,684	36.93%	106	0.59%	11,307	62.48%	18,097
Berkley	16,650	84.46%	131	0.66%	2,932	14.87%	19,713
Harrison	2,013	96.78%	----	--------	67	3.22%	2,080
Northumberland	**4,446**	**48.84%**	**197**	**2.16%**	**4,460**	**48.99%**	**9,103**
Randolph	932	98.00%	----	--------	19	2.00%	951
Rockingham	6,677	89.64%	----	--------	772	10.36%	7,449

The percentage of free persons of color in Northumberland County was slightly higher than the state average. When Northumberland was compared with her neighboring Northern Neck counties, enslaved persons out numbered whites. Free nonwhite persons made up little more than 1 to 2% of the total population in all the Northern Neck counties. Only in Northumberland were the number of enslaved persons and whites approximately equal. Northumberland had more free persons of color than Lancaster, however, percentage wise, Northumberland was second.

---

[15]Department of Commerce and Labor, Bureau of Census, S.N.D. North, Director, *Heads of Families at the First Census of the United States Taken in the Year 1790 -- Records of State Enumerations: 1782 to 1785 -- Virginia* (Washington, D.C.: Government Printing Office, 1908; rep. Baltimore: Genealogical Publishing Co., Inc., 1976), pp. 8, 9.

[16]Commerce Dept., *Heads of Families*, pp. 8-9.

[17]"Including Nottoway, a new county."

4

Richmond County had the least number of nonwhite persons in the Northern Neck. However, King George had the smallest percentage of free colored persons. Lancaster also had the smallest enslaved population, while Northumberland had the smallest percentage of nonwhite enslaved persons. (See Table 2).[18] Many of these counties contributed people for the Registers of Free Blacks in Northumberland County.

Table 2. Race and Status Breakdown of the 1790 Census for the Northern Neck Counties in Comparison with the State of Virginia.[19]							
Name of County	Number of Whites		Number of Nonwhites				Total Population
			Free		Enslaved persons		
	No.	% of Total	No.	% of Total	No.	% of Total	
King George	3,123	42.40%	86	**1.17%**	4,157	56.44%	7,366
Lancaster	2,259	40.07%	143	2.54%	**3,236**	57.40%	5,638
Northumberland	**4,446**	**48.84%**	**197**	**2.16%**	**4,460**	**48.99%**	**9,103**
Richmond	2,918	41.78%	**83**	1.19%	3,984	57.04%	6,985
Westmoreland	3,183	41.22%	114	1.48%	4,425	57.30%	7,722
NORTHERN NECK COUNTIES TOTAL	12,806	43.49%	537	1.82%	16,105	54.69%	29,448
STATE OF VIRGINIA	442,117	59.14%	12,866	1.72%	292,627	39.14%	747,610

---

[18]Commerce Dept., *Heads of Families*, p. 9.

[19]Commerce Dept., *Heads of Families*, pp. 8-9.

Some nonslave blacks did resort to petty thievery to survive. However, despite the fears of whites, so-called free blacks apparently committed only a few crimes. This is probably because their small community was very aware of the attitude of the surrounding whites. They were a close knit group, and probably realized that if one of them found trouble, the punishment would affect their whole community.[20]

There were many restrictions on nonslave blacks. European Americans greatly feared putting guns in the hands of African Americans -- free or enslaved. During the Colonial Wars their ultimate fear was that the enslaved persons would turn on them, and become their masters. A secondary consideration was that if allowed to fight, these captive laborers might simply disappear during the confusion of battle. Or worse, they could end up fighting for the enemy -- French, Spanish, or Native American.[21] How did whites come to this conclusion?

To ease their fears, whites began quickly to enact legislation to control their blacks. In January 1639, the Virginia House of Burgesses provided for everyone except Negroes to receive arms and ammunition. During the 1690's the General Assembly ordered militia officers not to enlist Negroes. Then blacks were forbidden to hold any military office. The same law forbade slaves to serve "in horse or foot." However, the legislation did not mention service on water. In 1705 Virginia's government excluded free black, mulatto, and Indian men from the militia throughout the colony, and these men were liable to pay a fine if they attended muster.[22] Also, in 1705, the law deprived so-called free blacks

---

20 Robert Anthony Wheeler, "Lancaster County, Virginia, 1650-1750: The Evolution of a Southern Tidewater Community" (Ph.D. Diss., Brown University, 1972), p. 144.

[21] Benjamin Quarles, "The Colonial Militia and Negro Manpower," *The Mississippi Valley Historical Review*, XLV (March 1959): pp. 644-645.

[22] Kathleen Mary Brown, "Gender and the Genesis of A Race and Class System in Virginia, 1630-1750" (Ph.D. diss., The University of Wisconsin -- Madison, 1990), pp. 403, 404; Barbara Lynn Doggett, "Parish Apprenticeship in Colonial Virginia: A Study of Northumberland County, 1680-1695 and 1750-1765" (M.A. thesis, College of William and Mary, 1981); Quarles, "Colonial Militia," pp. 644-645; June Purcel Guild, LLM. *Black Laws of Virginia: A Summary of the Legislative Acts of Virginia concerning Negroes from Earliest Times to the Present* (Whetter & Shepperson, 1936; reprint, New York: Negro Universities Press, 1969), p. 29.

of the right to hold office.[23] Further, only free black householders, or "licensed frontier dwellers could keep a gun, powder and shot" in 1705.[24] In 1723, the law prohibited free blacks from voting.[25] By 1738, free mulattoes, Negroes and Indians listed in the muster had to appear without arms, and be ready for 'servile labor' or work as drummers, trumpeters, or pioneers.[26]

---

[23]Carter G. Woodson, *Free Negro Heads of Families in the United States in 1830 together with a Brief Treatment of the Free Negro* (Washington: The Association for the Study of Negro Life and History, Inc., 1923), p. xxi.

[24]Brown, "Gender and Race," pp. 403, 404.

[25]Woodson, "Free Negro Heads of Families," p. xxi. Women were never allowed to vote.

[26]Brown, "Gender and Race," pp. 403, 404.

CHAPTER 2. THE NORTHUMBERLAND COUNTY REGISTER

Northumberland County lies in the eastern section of the Northern Neck of Virginia.[27] Today, the Northern Neck is the peninsula of land bordered by the Potomac River on the north, the Chesapeake Bay on the east, and the Rappahannock River on the south. Originally, it was part of Lord Fairfax's Northern Neck Proprietary, which extended from today's Northern Neck all the way to the Allegheny mountains. At its height, the Northern Neck Proprietary included the following counties: Prince George, Westmoreland, Northumberland, Richmond, Lancaster, Stafford, Prince William, Culpepper, Fauquier, Warren, and Frederick, and parts of Loudon, Fairfax, Clarke and Shenandoah.

In 1793, the Virginia General Assembly passed a law requiring all free blacks and mulattoes to go to their local courthouse to have their presence in the County registered, and to be given a number. The County Clerk recorded all registrations in books in his office. Such registration included each person's name, age, color, and the reason for, or the condition of their freedom. Each year, every registrant was to return to the courthouse to purchase a copy of his or her entry in the book at a cost of 25¢. Once every three years each registrant was to obtain a new certificate.[28] This certificate was to be kept on the person's body at all times when away from home. Failure to produce the certificate on demand from any white person was sufficient cause to be sold into slavery for failure to prove one's status as a free person of color. Therefore many free persons of color kept their certificates in water-resistant metal containers, which they carried on their person whenever leaving home. Many who were either always free (or freed during the seventeenth or early eighteenth centuries), owed their free status to the fact that the original freedmen's mothers were white. Herein are the names of approximately 674 different fpc's or free persons of color. The vast majority of the people on the Register were born free in Northumberland County. The second most common birthplace was Lancaster County, their southern neighbor. Running a distant third was Westmoreland County, Northumberland's northern neighbor. Two people were born in Richmond County [Martha Conway and Armistead Rich], and two were born in Essex County [Griffin Carpenter and Addison Drake]. One each was born in King & Queen County [Judith Rich] and Caroline County [Moses Pierce]. At least one was a first generation mulatto with a white mother [John Walker]. Two people on the list came to Northumberland with their former masters from Pennsylvania when slavery was outlawed there. One of that pair was an indentured servant [Polly]. The other was a freedman [Lear]. Their former owners manumitted the rest in their wills.

---

[27]Carolyn Jett, personal interview with writer, 17 September 1996; Introductory Speech of Carolyn Jett, given at the Meeting of the Northern Neck Genealogical Society, 17 September 1996. This area is now referred to as the lower Northern Neck. Lancaster County is also a part of the lower Northern Neck.

[28]Walter Biscoe R. Norris, ed. Westmoreland County, Virginia: 1653-1983 (Montross, VA: Westmoreland County Board of Supervisors, 1983), p. 550.

The categories on the first Register are: Registration Number, Name (Last Name First), Colour (complexion), Age (years or months), Stature (height), Marks or scars (which distinguished the individual), (whether the person was) Born Free or Emancipated, Date of Register (the date the person came to the courthouse to register), and When Certified (the date the Clerk of Court attested to the fact that this person was a fpc, and a resident of Northumberland County). In the second Register, the more common term height replaces the word stature. The reader will also notice a significant difference between how much information is given in the first register, and that in the subsequent one. Also, about half of the first page was missing by the time this writer obtained a copy for transcription. Some of the missing information was added based on subsequent entries. Figure 1 shows an example of a Freedom Certificate from Lancaster County. The Northumberland County certificates are similar to this certificate, and the Lancaster County Register is similar to this register.

Figure 1. Freedom Certificate of Susan Nicken, Lancaster County, Virginia. "1857 Feby 17"

Key:

General

? = handwriting illegible

?^{M} = part of page missing

[ns] = name supplied from subsequent registration. superscript number is number of subsequent registration. This page and number are missing from the original.

[nln] = no last name given

Blank cells are blank on the original.

Column Headings

P# = Page Number

Reg. # = Number on the Register

BF or Eman = Born Free or Emancipated

When Cert. = When Certified by the Court

Colour

abm^m = a bright mulatto

aNm = a Negro man

bm = black man

b^{r}b = bright boy

b^{r}m = bright man

bm^u = bright mulatto

b^{r}mw = bright mulatto woman

bw = black woman

b^{r}w = bright woman

db = dark boy

dg = dark girl

dl = dark lad

dtb = dark tawney boy

do = ditto

dw = dark woman

lm = light man

lm^u = light mulatto

m^{u}b = mulatto boy

m^{u}m = mulatto man

m^{u}w = mulatto woman

Ng = Negro girl

Nm = Negro man

Age

y = year(s), yo = years old

yoa = years of age, m = months

c. = about, n. = nearly

IITA = Infant in the Arms

up = upwards

[ ] = number in brackets calculated based upon subsequent information

Stature

' = feet

" = inches

h = high

Marks or Scars

namos = no apparent mark or scar

nfmx = no flesh marks exposed

nmos = no mark or scar

npfm = no particular flesh marks

npm = no particular mark

npsom = no particular scars or marks

nrm = no remarkable scars

nsom = no scar or mark

nsoom = no scars or other marks

nsoorm = no scars or other remarkable marks

BF or Eman

BF = Born Free

BoD = Born of Ditto

Do = Ditto

BF^L = Born of Free Parents in Lancaster County

BF^N = Born of Free Parents in Northumberland County

Eman = Emancipated

IS = Indentured Servant

West^d = Westmoreland

Date of Register/When Cert.

c&d = Certified & delivered

ctbc = certified to be correct

E&c = Examined & certified

E&fc = Examined & found correct

E&fcbtc = Examined & found correct by the court

Ebtc = Examined by the court

Ebtc&fc = Examined by the court & found correct

Re&fc = Register examined & found correct

Jany = January

Feb = February

Mar = March

Ap^l = April

Aug = August, Agust = August

Augst = August

Sept = September

Oct = October, Octr = October

Oct^o = October   Decb = December

PART I: 1803-1810

P #	Reg. #	Name, Last	Name, First	Colour	Age	Stature	Marks or scars	BF or EMAN	Date of Register	When Certified
		"Northumberland County, Virginia, Register of Free Negroes, 1803-1849." **PART I: 1803-1810**								
1	1									
1	2									
1	3	Bee [ns][92, 106]	Charlotte							
1	4									
1	5	Black [ns][62]	Robt.							
1	6	Mason [ns][37]	Chloe							
1	7									
1	8									
1	9									
1	10									
1	11									
1	12									
1	13									
1	14									
1	15									
1	16	Bee [ns][94]	Lucy							
2	17	Peters	John	Tawney	c. 17 yoa	5' 3"	a scar on the breast[1]	BF	13th Jany 1806	E&fc[2]
2	18	[missing number]								

"Northumberland County, Virginia, Register of Free Negroes, 1803-1849."
PART I: 1803-1810

P #	Reg. #	Name, Last	Name, First	Colour	Age	Stature	Marks or scars	BF or EMAN	Date of Register	When Certified
2	19	Day	Presley	bm	c. 18 y	5' 6¼" h	small scar on his left wrist	BF	10 Feby 1806	
2	20	Day[181]	Sam	Black	n, 15 y	5' 4" h	nflmx	BF	10 March 1806	
2	21	Boyd	James	bm	c. 19 y	5' 5"	nflmx	BF	10 March 1806	
2	22	Johnston	James C.	dm	19 y & up	5' 5¼"	a scar on the left hand[3]	BF	10 March 1806	
2	23	Nicken	John	bm	12 y	4' 7½"	nsoom	BF	10 March 1806	
2	24	Causey	Polly	bm	25 y	5' 5"	nsoom	BF	12 March 1806	E&fc[4]
2	25	[nln]	Charlotte	Black	c. 25 y	5' 3½" h	nsoom	Eman[5]	18 May 1806	E&fc[6]
2	26	[nln]	Moses	mulatto	c. 26 y	5' 11"	nsoom	same	9 June 1806	E&fc[7]
2	27	Causey	William	mulatto	c. 60 y	5' 9¼"	scar on left arm[8]	BF	12 Jany 1807	
2	28	Causey	Nelly	abm	c. 48 y	5' 3"	a scar on the right arm[9]	BF	2d Mar. 1807	
2	29	Toulson	Betty	bw	c. 33 y	5' 3½"	nsoom	BF	12 March 1806	E&fc[1]
2	30	Causey	Rachel	dm	c. 52 y	5' 2"	scar on right from burn[11]	Eman[1²]	9th March 1807	E&fc[1]
2	31	Anderwig?	Lancelot	bm	c. 30 y	5' 8"	pitted with small pox[14]	BF[15]	14 Sep 1807	E&fc[1]
2	32	[nln]	Maces	mulatto	c. 27 y	5' 11"	nsoom	Eman[1]	14 Sep[t] 1807	
2	33	[nln]	Polly	bw	28 y	5' 1¾" h	a scar on the forehead	IS[18]	5 April 1808	E&fc[?m]
3	34	Bee	Lucy	bw	25 y	5' 2½" h	?M	?M	?M	?M

P #	Reg. #	Name, Last	Name, First	Colour	Age	Stature	Marks or scars	BF or EMAN	Date of Register	When Certified
							"Northumberland County, Virginia, Register of Free Negroes, 1803-1849." **PART I: 1803-1810**				
3	35	Bee [16, 61]	Janey	black[19]	17 y	5' 2¼" h	?[M]	?[M]	?[M] 09	?[M]
3	36	Bee	Sally	bg	14 y	5' 2½" h	?[M]	?[M]	9 Jany 1809	
3	37[29]	Mason[6]	Chloe	b[r]m	c. 24	5' 8¾" h[30]	?	?[M]	9 Jany 1809	
3	38	Bee	Charlotte	bw	23 y	5' 2¼" h	?[M]	?[M]	9 Jany 1809	
3	39	Bee[75]	Shadrach	bm	20 y	5' 9¼" h	?[M]	?[M]	9 Jany 1809	
3	40	Boyd	Wm	b[r]m	22 y	5' 11" h	?[M]	?[M]	13 march 1809	
3	41	Toulson	Polly	b[r]m	c. 18	5' 2" h	?[M]	?[M]	13 march 1809	
3	42	Campbell	Eliza	b[r]m	c. 30	5' 3½" h	?[M]	?[M]	8 May 1809	E&fc[2]$_0$
3	43	Nicken	Amos	bm	c. 34	5' 8½" h	?[M]	?[M]	12 June 1809	E&fc[2]$_1$
3	44	Weaver	Hosea	dtb	c. 17	5' 5½" h	?[M]	?[M]	10 Oct 1809[22]	E&fc[23]
3	45	Weaver[254]	Sally	bw	c. 36	5' 5½" h	?[M]	?[M]	6 July 1810	E&fc[24]
3	[46]	Causey	Chaplain	b[r]m	c. 16	5' ½" h	?[M]	?[M]	14 Augt 1810	
3	[47]	Causey[90]	Lucretia	bw	c. 22	5' ¾" h	?[M]	?[M]	14 Aug 1810	
3	[48]	Peters	John	dm[u]	c. 21	5' 7½" h	?[M]	?[M]	8 Octr 1810	E&fc[25]
3	49	Thomas	Mary	b[r]mw	19 y	5' 5½" h	?	?	14 Nov. 1810	
3	50	Thomas	Charlotte	b[r]m	c. 26 y	5' 7" h	?[M]	?[M]	14 Nov 1810	

[29]Formerly registered No. 6.

[30]5 feet 8¾ inches high -- having 5 children.

16

"Northumberland County, Virginia, Register of Free Negroes, 1803-1849." **PART I: 1803-1810**										
P #	Reg. #	Name, Last	Name, First	Colour	Age	Stature	Marks or scars	BF or EMAN	Date of Register	When Certified
3	51	Dudley[59]	John	mulatto	c. 22 yoa	5' 5¾" h	?M	?M	10 Dec 1810	

PART II: 1811-1820

				"Northumberland County, Virginia, Register of Free Negroes, 1803-1849." PART II: 1811-1820					
P #	Reg. #	Name, Last	Name, First	Colour	Age	Stature	Marks or scars	BF or EMAN	Date of Register	When Certified
3	[54]	Causey[65]	John	dl	c. 20	5' 7⅛"h	?[M]	?[M]	12 Augst 1811	E&fc[26]
3	55	Causey[63]	Wm. [ns]	m"m	24 y	5' 5½" h	?[M]	?[M]	12 Augt 1811	
4?[M]	56?[M]	[nln]	Lear [ns][79]	?[M] [c. 24]	?[M]	?[M]	a scar on the right side of neck	Eman[27]	1811 Oct° 14	
4[28]	57	Toulson[80]	Betty	bw	c. 37 y	?[m]	scar on the right side forehead[29]	BF[N]	11th Nov. 1811	
4	58	[nln]	Tom	bm	c. 27 y	?[m]	small not on the left side forehead[30]	Eman[31]	31 Dec[r] 1811	E&fc[32]
4	59[31]	Dudley[51]	John	mulatto	23 yoa	5 ?[m]	a scar in the right groin	BF[N]	13 Jany 1812	E&fc[33]
4	60	Fletcher	George W.	mulatto	25 yoa	5 ?[m]	a scar on left arm below elbow	BF[N]	10 March 1812	
4	61[32]	Bee[16, 35]	Jane	bw	c. 20 yo	5 ?[m]	npm	BF[N]	13 July 1812	c&d[34]
4	62[33]	Black[5]	Robt.	dm"	c. 30	5 ?[m]	scar between thumb/forefinger[35]	BF[N]	11 Aug[t] 1812	c&d[36]
4	63[34]	Causey[55]	Wm.	m"m	c. 25 yoa	5?[M]	marked on left wrist with India Ink[37]	BF[N]	12 Oct° 1812	cert[d38]

[31]No. 59 formerly registered no. 51.

[32]No. 61 formerly No. 35.

[33]No. 62 formerly No. 5.

[34]No. 63 formerly No. 55.

	**"Northumberland County, Virginia, Register of Free Negroes, 1803-1849."** **PART II: 1811-1820**

P #	Reg. #	Name, Last	Name, First	Colour	Age	Stature	Marks or scars	BF or EMAN	Date of Register	When Certified
4	64[35]	[nln]	Moses[32]	bm"	c. 32 yo	5 ?M	nsoom	Eman[39]	9 Nov 1812	
4	65[36]	Causey[54]	John	dark lad	c. 21 yoa	5'	nsoorm	BF[N]	8th Jan 1813	ctbc[40]
4	66	[nln]	Winney	bw	c. 60 yoa	5' ?M	small scar over the right temple [41]	Eman[42]	11th Jan 1813	
4	67	[nln]	Tom	a Nm	c. 19 y	5'	small scar under right eye near[43]	Eman[44]	14 June 1813	c&d[45]
4	68	Thomas	Milly	Ng	c. 16 y	5'	scar on inside of right? breast[46]	BF[N]	8th Jan 1813	ctbc[47]
4	69	Bee	Isaac	Nm	c. 26[5] y	5'	left hand much injured by a burn[48]	BF[N]	13 Sept. 1813	
4	70	Peters[88]	Joseph	dm"	c. 21 y	5' ?M	scar one right side of his head.[49]	BF[N]	10 Jan 1814	ctbc[50]
4	71	Bee	Gabriel	bm	c.	5' ?M	A scar between the eyes	BF[N]	30 July 1814	
4	72[51]	Peters	Molly	lm"	c. 46 y	5'	black mark / mole left arm [52]	BF[L]	30 July 1814	E&c[53]
4	73[54]	?M [ns] Toulson[104]	?M Betty	?M			a scar between the eyes	BF[N]	30 July 1814	
4	74	?M	?M	?M						
4	73	Toulson[104]	Patty [Betty]	Bw	c. 20 yo	5' h	small black spot over right eye.[55]	BF[N]	30th July 1814	
5	74	Causey	Tho.	mulatto	20 y	5' 6¾"	scar on fleshy part right leg[56]	BF[N]	30 July 1814	

---

[35]No. 64 formerly No. 32.

[36]No. 65 formerly No. 54.

	**"Northumberland County, Virginia, Register of Free Negroes, 1803-1849."** **PART II: 1811-1820**
P #	Reg. #	Name, Last	Name, First	Colour	Age	Stature	Marks or scars	BF or EMAN	Date of Register	When Certified
5	75[37]	Bee[39]	Shadrach	bm	c. 25 y	5' 8¾"	a small scar on the left wrist.	BF^N	30 July 1814	
5	76	Peters	Sally	mulatto	c. 17 y	5' 5½"	npsom	BF^L	1s Aug 1814	
5	77	Peters	Charles	mulatto	c. 24 y	5' 5¾"	a long scar on his right arm	BF^L	1 Augt 1814	
5	78	Day	Winney	mulatto	c. 55 y	5' ½"	a wart over her left eye	BF^N	1 Augt 1814	
5	79[38]	[nln]	Lear[56]	Bw	c. 27 y	4' 11½"	scar on the right side of neck[57]	Eman[58]	1 Aug 1814	
5	80[39]	Toulson[57, 95]	Betty	bw	c. 40 y	5' 2¾"	small scar underside right arm[59]	BF^N	1 Aug 1814	
5	81	Toulson	Sally	bw	c. 36 y	5' 4¾"	npm	BF^N	1 Augt	
5	82	Day	Winney the younger	bw	c. 22 y	5' 2¼"	npm	BF^N	1 Aug 1814	
5	83	Thomas	Amey	m^{n}w	c. 36 y	5' 3½"	small scar inn side right arm[60]	BF^N	2 Aug 1814	
5	84	Thomas	Sally	bm	c. 20 y	5' 1"	small scar on back left hand[61]	BF^N	14 Nov 1814	
5	85	Toulson[97, 183, 201]	Eliz. A.	bm	c. 21 y	5' 8½"	burn on back right hand[62]	BF^N	16 Nov 1814	
5	86	Redman	George	Nm	c. 38 y	5' 8"	small scar on back left hand[63]	Eman[64]	13 Feb 1815	9 Oct[65]

[37]75 formerly No. 39.

[38]79 formerly 56.

[39]80 formerly [57].

"Northumberland County, Virginia, Register of Free Negroes, 1803-1849."
PART II: 1811-1820

P #	Reg. #	Name, Last	Name, First	Colour	Age	Stature	Marks or scars	BF or EMAN	Date of Register	When Certified
5	87	Sorrell[720]	Edward	bm	c. 21 y	5' 10"	scar on the left ankle & on the shin.	BF[N]	8th May 1815	E& fc[66]
5	88[40]	Peters[70, 709]	Joseph	dm	c. 22 y	5' 10⅛"	scar on right side his head	BF[N]	12 June 1815	E&fc[67]
5	89	Walker	John	dm	c. 24 yo	5' 7"	a scar on his right side	BF[68]	12 June 1815	
5	90[69]	Causey[47]	Lukey	bw	c. 24 y	5' 4"	Lost 2 upper fore teeth	BF[N]	12 June 1815	
5	91[70]	Bee	Shadrach	bm	c. 26 y	5' 8¾"	small scar in the left wrist	BF[N]	14 Aug 1815	
5	92[41]	?M[3, 106]			c. 28	same[71]	same	same	12 Jany 1818	Re&fc[72]
6	91	Causey	Tho.	bm	22 yo	5' 9"h	no scar	BF[N]	11 Sept 1815	11 Sept[73]
6	92[74]	Bee[3]	Charlotte	bw	c. 31 y	5' 3"	a scar on the left arm.	BF[N]	26 Apl 1816	
6	93	Bee[107]	Louisa	bg	13 y	4' 9½"	No particular marks.	do	26 Apl 1816	
6	94[42]	Bee[16, 108]	Lucy	dw	35 y	5' 7" h	space between teeth.[75]	do	14 May 1816	
6	95[43]	Toulson[80]	Betty	bw	c. 24 yo	5' 2¾"	small scar underside right arm[76]	do	10 June 1816	Re[77]

---

[40]88 formerly 70.

[41]92 formerly 3.

[42]94 formerly 16.

[43]95 formerly 80.

**"Northumberland County, Virginia, Register of Free Negroes, 1803-1849."** **PART II: 1811-1820**											

P #	Reg. #	Name, Last	Name, First	Colour	Age	Stature	Marks or scars	BF or EMAN	Date of Register	When Certified
6	96	Toulson	Nelly	dw	c. 30 yo	6' h	a scar on the right breast	do	10 June 1816	Re&fc[78]
6	97[44]	Toulson[85, 183, 201]	Eliz. A.	bw	c. 23 yo	5' 8½" h	a burn on the back of right hand	do	10 June 1816	
6	98	Toulson	John	dm	c. 28 yo	6' h	a scar over the right eye.	do	10 June 1816	E[79]
6	99	Johnston	Ann	dm[u]	c. 28 y	5' 5¼" h	no particular scars	do	8 July 1816	Re&fc[80]
6	100	Bee	Peggy	dw	c. 18 y	5' 7½" h	nmod	do	11 Nov. 1816	
6	101	Bee	Molly	do	c. 20	4' 11" h	flesh mole between her breasts	do	11 Nov. 1816	
6	102	Ball	Griffin	bm[u]	16 y	5' 7" h	no particular	Eman[81]	26 Feb 1817	Re&fc[82]
6	103	[nln]	Winney	bw		5' h	a mark from cut of ax[83]	Eman[84]	8 Mar 1817	Re&fc[85]
6	104[45]	Toulson[73]	Patty	bw	c. 23 y	5' ¾" h	a small black spot near right eye	BF[N]	2 Ap[l] 1817	
6	105	Toulson	Tom	bm[u]	19 y	5' 8½"	scar middle finger left hand[86]	BF[N]	14 July 1817	Re&fc[87]
6	106[88]	Bee[3, 92]	Charlotte	bw	c. 32 y	5' 3" h	a scar on the left arm.	BF[N]	14 July 1817	Re&fc[89]
6	107[46]	Bee[93]	Louisa	bg	14 y	4' 11½"	npm	do	14 July 1817	Re&fc[90]

[44]97 formerly 85.

[45]106 formerly 73.

[46]107 formerly 93.

P #	Reg. #	Name, Last	Name, First	Colour	Age	Stature	Marks or scars	BF or EMAN	Date of Register	When Certified
						"Northumberland County, Virginia, Register of Free Negroes, 1803-1849." **PART II: 1811-1820**				
6	108	Bee[16, 94]	Lucy	dw	36 y	5' 7"	space between upper foreteeth[91]	do		Re&fc[92]
6	109	Carpenter	Whittington	bm[u]	21 y	5' 8½" h	npsom	do	13 Oct° 1817	Re&fc[93]
7	110	[nln]	Lear	bw	c. 31 y	4' 11½"	scar on right side of neck[94]	Eman[95]	12th May 1818	
7	111	Day	Nancy Taylor	bm[u]	c. 19 y	5' 3"	small scar on right wrist[96]	BF[N]	6 June 1818	Re&fc[97]
7	112	Carpenter	Spencer	db	c. 15 y	5' 1½"	small scar in left eye brow[98]	BF[N]	8 June	Re&fc[99]
7	113	Ball	Griffin	bm[u]	c. 17 y	5' 8¼"	npmos	Eman[100]	11 Augst	Re&fc[101]
7	114	Thomas	Mary	dm[u]	c. 23 y	5' h	npmos	BF[N]	20th Oct[r]	E&fc
7	115	Toulson[125, 172, 187]	Patty	bw	c. 24 y	5' ¾"	small black spot near right eye[102]	BF[N]	14 Dec[b] 1818	
7	116	Ball[150]	Hiram	bm[u]	c. 17 y	5' 5¾" h	npmos	Eman[103]	19 March 1819	
7	117	Weaver	Hosea	dm[u]	c. 25 y	5' 7½"	small wattle near right ear.[104]	BF[N]	8th Feby	E&fc
7	118	Wells[192]	Lucy	bw	c. 37 yo	5'1" h	npmos	Eman[105]	19 March 1819	
7	119	Day	Judy	dm[u]	c. 53 yo	5' 3"	a flesh mould on back of neck.[106]	BF[N]	17 April 1819	E&fc
7	120	Day	Judy Jr.[47]	bw	c. 40 y	5' 3¼" h	npsom	BF[N]	10 May	E&fc
7	120	Day[107]	James		[9 y]					
7	120	Day[108]	Polly		[bet. 9-2]					
7	120	Day[109]	Sally		[bet. 9-2]					

[47]Presented her children James, Polly, Sally & Betsy between the ages of 9 & 2.

[48] daughter of the above.

"Northumberland County, Virginia, Register of Free Negroes, 1803-1849."
PART II: 1811-1820

P #	Reg. #	Name, Last	Name, First	Colour	Age	Stature	Marks or scars	BF or EMAN	Date of Register	When Certified
7	120	Day[110]	Betsy		[2 y]					
7	121	Day	Harriet[48]	dg	c. 12 y	5' 2½" h	same	same	10 Ma	E&fc
8	122	Hall	Polly	bm"	21 yo	5' ½"	npm	BF[111]	10 July 1819	E&fc[112]
8	123	Toulson	Sally	bw	c. 38 yo	5' 4¾"	npm	BF[N]	27th Jany 1820	
8	124	Toulson	Billy	bm"	c. 19 yo	5' 11¾"	right eye out no other marks[113]	BF[N]	20th Mar. 1820	
8	125[114]	Toulson[115, 172, 187]	Patty	bw	c. 25 y	5' 1" h	a small black spot near right eye	BF[N]	13 June 1820	Reg&fc[115]
8	126	Jones[180]	Griffin	m"m	c. 23 y	6' 3½"	forefinger right hand scared[116]	BF[N]	10 July 1820	
8	127	Dudley	Harriet	bm"	18 yo	5' ½"	scar across right lower lip[117]	BF[N]	11 Sept 1820	

PART III: 1821-1830

P #	Reg. #	Name, Last	Name, First	Colour	Age	Stature	Marks or scars	BF or EMAN	Date of Register	When Certified
						"Northumberland County, Virginia, Register of Free Negroes, 1803-1849." PART III: 1821-1830				
8	130	Day[49]	Spencer	m^{u}b	16 yoa	5' 1" h	scar near right eye[118]	BF^N	16 May 1821	E&fc[119]
8	131	Day	James Stokely[50]	mulatto	12 yoa	4' 8" h	slight mark on the left side of his neck	BF^N	16 May 1821	E&fc
8	132	Day	Sally	b^{r}m	26 yo	5' 6" h	npm	BF^N	16 may 1821	E&fc
8	133	Day	Lucy	b^{r}m	19 yo	5' 3" h	npm	same	16 May 1822	E&fc
8	134	Causey	Lukey	bw	c. 25 y	5' 1" h	has lost her foreteeth	BF^N	15 Augt 1821	E&fc
8	135	Nicken	Abraham	bm	33 y	5' 10" h	small scar on the right side of his face	BF^N	12 Nov 1821	E&fc
8	136	Day	Wm	bm	19 y	5' 7½" h	a small scar on the right eyebrow	BF^N	11 March 1822	E&fc
8	137	Day[263]	Jane	m^{u}w	c. 47 y	5' 3" h	npm	BF^N	11 Mar 1822	E&fc
8	138	Weaver	Austin	bm	c. 17 y	6' h	npm	BF^N	11 mar 1822	
9	139	[nln]	Charlotte	bw	c. 38 yoa	5'1½" h				
9	140	Hancock[51]	Vincent	bm	19 yoa	5' 6½" h				

[49]Spencer Day son of Judy.

[50]James Stokely Day son of Judy Day.

[51]Son of the above. [Charlotte]

P #	Reg. #	Name, Last	Name, First	Colour	Age	Stature	Marks or scars	BF or EMAN	Date of Register	When Certified
						"Northumberland County, Virginia, Register of Free Negroes, 1803-1849." PART III: 1821-1830				
9	141	[nln]	Fanny[52]	bw	c. 15 y	5'				
9	142	[nln]	Patty[53]	bg	c. 13 y	4' 1½"				
9	143	[nln]	Royston[54]	abb	c. 10 y	4' 5½"				
9	144	[nln]	Sally[55]	yellow	5 mo					
9	145	Day	Jane	m^{u}w	20 yo	5' 2¾" h				
9	146	Sank	Spencer	bm	c. 24 yo	5' 7½" h				
9	147	Bee[210, 235]	Vincent	bm	21 yoa	5' 7" h				
9	148	Nickins	Linsey	bm	23 yoa	5' 10" h	burn on left hand bet thumb[120]	Eman[121]	8 April 1822	E&fc[122]
9	149	Ball	Eliza W.	bm^u	18 yo	5' 3" h				
9	150[123]	Ball[116]	Hiram	bm^u	c. 21 yo	5' 11" h				
9	151	Ball	Wm	bm^u	16 yo	4' 9½"				
9	152	Ball	Louisa	do	15 y	5' 2"				
9	153	Ball[56]	Nancy	bm^u	13 y					

[52]Also a daughter of Charlotte.

[53]Also daughter of Charlotte.

[54]A son of Charlotte.

[55]Daughter of Fanny an infant.

[56]Children of Rosa all bright mulattoes. [Nancy, Mottrom, Lucy, and Judy Ball]

	**"Northumberland County, Virginia, Register of Free Negroes, 1803-1849."** **PART III: 1821-1830**
P #	Reg. #	Name, Last	Name, First	Colour	Age	Stature	Marks or scars	BF or EMAN	Date of Register	When Certified
9	153	Ball	Mottrom	bm[u]	10 y					
9	153	Ball	Lucy	bm[u]	9 y					
9	153	Ball	Judy	bm[u]	7 y					
9	154	Thomas	Spencer	bm	23 y	6' 3"				
9	155	Spriddle	Steptoe	bm	21 y	5' 10"				
9	156	Day	Harriot	dg	17 y	5' 4½"				
10	157	Ball	Rose[57]	bw	36 y	5' 7"	nmos	Eman[124]	13 May 1823	E&fc[125]
10	157[58]	Ball	Griffin	light						
10	157[59]	Ball	Hiram[60]	light						
10	157[61]	Ball	Elisa W.[62]	light						

[57]Having the following children composing her family to wit -- Griffin, Hiram, Elisa W., W^m, Louisa, Nancy, Lucy, Mottrom, Judy all of light complexion.

[58]Name not arranged in this manner in the original.

[59]Name not arranged in this manner in the original.

[60]Having the following children composing her family to wit -- Griffin, Hiram, Elisa W., W^m, Louisa, Nancy, Lucy, Mottrom, Judy all of light complexion.

[61]Name not arranged in this manner in the original.

[62]Having the following children composing her family to wit -- Griffin, Hiram, Elisa W., W^m, Louisa, Nancy, Lucy, Mottrom, Judy all of light complexion.

	**"Northumberland County, Virginia, Register of Free Negroes, 1803-1849."** **PART III: 1821-1830**
P #	Reg. #	Name, Last	Name, First	Colour	Age	Stature	Marks or scars	BF or EMAN	Date of Register	When Certified
10	157[63]	Ball	W[m64]	light						
10	157[65]	Ball	Louisa[66]	light						
10	157[67]	Ball	Nancy[68]	light						
10	157[69]	Ball	Lucy[70]	light						

---

[63]Name not arranged in this manner in the original.

[64]Having the following children composing her family to wit -- Griffin, Hiram, Elisa W., W[m], Louisa, Nancy, Lucy, Mottrom, Judy all of light complexion.

[65]Name not arranged in this manner in the original.

[66]Having the following children composing her family to wit -- Griffin, Hiram, Elisa W., W[m], Louisa, Nancy, Lucy, Mottrom, Judy all of light complexion.

[67]Name not arranged in this manner in the original.

[68]Having the following children composing her family to wit -- Griffin, Hiram, Elisa W., W[m], Louisa, Nancy, Lucy, Mottrom, Judy all of light complexion.

[69]Name not arranged in this manner in the original.

[70]Having the following children composing her family to wit -- Griffin, Hiram, Elisa W., W[m], Louisa, Nancy, Lucy, Mottrom, Judy all of light complexion.

[71] Name not arranged in this manner in the original.

[72] Having the following children composing her family to wit -- Griffin, Hiram, Elisa W., W^m, Louisa, Nancy, Lucy, Mottrom, Judy all of light complexion.

[73] Name not arranged in this manner in the original.

[74] Having the following children composing her family to wit -- Griffin, Hiram, Elisa W., W^m, Louisa, Nancy, Lucy, Mottrom, Judy all of light complexion.

"Northumberland County, Virginia, Register of Free Negroes, 1803-1849."
PART III: 1821-1830

P #	Reg. #	Name, Last	Name, First	Colour	Age	Stature	Marks or scars	BF or EMAN	Date of Register	When Certified
10	157[71]	Ball	Mottrom[72]	light						
10	157[73]	Ball	Judy[74]	light						
10	158	Watkins	Lindsey L.	m"m	22 y	5' 9" h	a scar on the right hand	BF[N]	9th June 1823	E&fc[126]
10	159	Kelly	John	dm"m	18 y	5' 5"	s scar on the left leg	same	same	E&fc[127]
10	160	Wiggins	Ann	dw	48 y	5'	a small scar on the right hand	same	same	E&fc[128]
10	161	Jones	Williamson	bm	c. 25 y	5' 5"	scar on nose & between eyes[129]	same	17 June 1823	E&fc[130]
10	162	Carpenter	Molly	m"w	48 y	5' 5"	a scar on the left hand	same	17 June 1823	
10	163	Carpenter	Robert	bm	c. 19 y	5' 4½"	a small scar over the right eye.	same	17 June 1823	
10	164	Carpenter	Mary	m"g	15 yo	5' 2"	nompu	BF[31]	12 July 1823	

"Northumberland County, Virginia, Register of Free Negroes, 1803-1849."
PART III: 1821-1830

P #	Reg. #	Name, Last	Name, First	Colour	Age	Stature	Marks or scars	BF or EMAN	Date of Register	When Certified
10	165	Carpenter	Nancy	dw	19 yo	5' 1½"	a scar on each breast	BF[132]	12 July 1823	
10	166	Carpenter	Benj[a]	bm	29 y	5' 11½"	nvmos	same	14 Oct 1823	
10	167	Ball	Griffin	m[u]m	23 y	5' 10"	nsom	Eman[133]	12 Jan 1824	E&c[134]
10	168	Townsend or Burk	Ellen	bw	c. 20	5' 3"	no scars	BF	6 Feb. 1824	E&c[135]
10	169	Laws	Patsy	bw	c. 25	5' h	a scar on the right hand	BF	3rd March 1824	
10	170	Jones[177]	Armistead	bm[u]	c. 22 y	5' 7½" h	a scar on the right side of the face	BF[N136]	8 March 1824	
10	171	Sorrel	W[m]	m[ub]	c. 20 y	5' 7" h	nmos	BF	8th March 1824	E&c[137]
10	172[75]	Toulson[125, 187]	Patty	bw	c. 29 y	5' 1"	small black spot near right eye[138]	BF	31st Mar. 1824	
10	173	Wells	Judy	bw	c. 29 y	5' 1¾" h	no remarkable scar	BF	10 Apr 1824	
10	174	Nickens	Hiram	m[u]b	c. 22 y	5' 7½" h	letters HN on left arm & anchor[139]	BF[N]	10 May 1824	E&c[140]
10	175	Sank	Holland	m[u]m	c. 22 y	5' 6½" h	ncsom	BF[N]	10 May 1824	E&c[141]

[75]172 formerly 125.

	"Northumberland County, Virginia, Register of Free Negroes, 1803-1849." PART III: 1821-1830

P #	Reg. #	Name, Last	Name, First	Colour	Age	Stature	Marks or scars	BF or EMAN	Date of Register	When Certified
10	176	Day[76]	Judy	bw	c. 44 y	5' ¾"	npm	do	11 Oct° 1824	Ebc&ctbc[142]
10	176[77]	Day	James		[13]					
10	176[78]	Day	Polly[143]		[13 - 6]					
10	176[79]	Day	Sally[144]		[13 - 6]					
10	176[80]	Day	Betsy[145]		[6]					
11	177[81]	Jones[170]	Armistead	bm[u]	c. 23 y	5' 7½"	small scar on right side of face	BF[N146]	14 March 1825	Ebc&fc[147]
11	178	[missing number]								
11	179	Weaver	Abraham	mulatto	18 y	5' 7½""	small scar over right eye	BF[N]	21 March 1825	E&fc[148]
11	180[82]	Jones[126]	Griffin	m[u]m	28 y	6' 2¼"	forefinger right hand scarred[149]	same	10 May 1825	Ebc[150]

[76]Judy Day is presented her children James Polly Sally & Betty between the ages of 13 & 6.

[77]Name does not appear in this manner in the original.

[78]Name does not appear in this manner in the original.

[79]Name does not appear in this manner in the original.

[80]Name does not appear in this manner in the original.

[81]177 formerly 170.

[82]180 formerly 126.

33

P #	Reg. #	Name, Last	Name, First	Colour	Age	Stature	Marks or scars	BF or EMAN	Date of Register	When Certified
11	181[83]	Day[20]	Saml F.	black	34 y	5' 9½" h	several scars on left side his face.[151]	same	26 May 1825	
11	182	Toulson[215]	James	mulatto	21 y	5' 8½" h	small scar on his right side	same	9 Sept 1825	Ebc[152]
11	183[84]	Toulson[97, 85]	Eliz A.	mulatto	23 y	5' 1" h	scar on the right arm.	same	12th Sept 1825	Ebc[153]
11	184	Nicken	Sukey	black	27 y	5' 5" h	lost a foretooth above	BF[N]	12 Sept 1825	Ebc&fc[154]
11	185	Nicken	Cyrus	black	21 y	5' 9½" h	a scar on the right arm	same	12 Sept 1825	
11	186	Nicken	Betsy	black	16 y	5' 2" h	npm	same	12 Sept 1825	
11	187[85]	Toulson[125, 172]	Patty	black	c. 21	5' 1"	small spot near the right eye.	same	13 March 1826	E&fc[155]
11	188	Bell	John	black	22	5' 8" h	small black spot on the right side.	BF[L]	29 March 1826	
11	189	Jones	Wade	bm[u]	c. 20	5' 8½" h	somewhat freckled near his nose.	BF[N]	9th May 1826	Ebc&fc[156]
11	190	Carpenter	Griffin	black	c. 24	5' 3" h	a scar on the left leg	BF[157]	11 July 1826	

[83]181 formerly 20.

[84]183 formerly 97 & 85.

[85]187 formerly 125 & 172.

"Northumberland County, Virginia, Register of Free Negroes, 1803-1849."
PART III: 1821-1830

P #	Reg. #	Name, Last	Name, First	Colour	Age	Stature	Marks or scars	BF or EMAN	Date of Register	When Certified
11	191	Spriddle	Betsy	dm^u	c. 24 y	5' 5¼"	small scar on the chinn	BF^N	11 Sept 1826	Eboo&fc[158]
11	192[86]	Wells[118]	Lucy	bw	c. 34 y	5' 1" h	npmos	Eman[159]	19 Sept 1826	E&fc[160]
11	193	Conway	Martha	dg	12 y	4' 9"	nmos	BF[161]	19 Sept 1826	
11	194	Day	William	dm^u	c. 22	5' 5"	a scar on the left arm.	BF^N	1 Oct^o 1826	
11	195	[nln]	James[245]	bm	31 y	5' 6"	a scar on the left are	Eman[162]	6 Oct^o 1826	Eboo&fc[163]
11	196?^{M}	Nicken	Betsy	black	17 y	5' 2"	namos	BF^N	9 Oct^o 1826	E&fc[164]
12	197	[nln]	Lucy[249]	dw	21 y	5'	namos	Eman[165]	13 Nov 1826	Exam^d[166]
12	198	Toulson	Granville	m^{u}m	21 y	5' 8½" h	namos	BF^N	11 Feb. 1827	E&fc[167]
12	199	Sorrel	James	bm^u	17	5' 6½" h	namos	BF^N	12 Feb 1827	E&ctbc[168]
12	200	Boyd	Lucy	bm^u	25	5' 8" h	a scar on the right arm	same	3 Apl 1827	E&fc[169]

35

P #	Reg. #	Name, Last	Name, First	Colour	Age	Stature	Marks or scars	BF or EMAN	Date of Register	When Certified
							"Northumberland County, Virginia, Register of Free Negroes, 1803-1849." PART III: 1821-1830			
12	201[87]	Toulson[83, 85, 97, 201]	Eliz. A.[88]	mulatto	c. 26	5' 1"	has a scar on her right arm.	same	9 May 1827	E&fc[170]
12	201	Toulson	Ann	mulatto	8 yoa					
12	202	Jones	Henrietta	mulatto	32 y	5' 2"	scars on her left arm above elbow	same	11 June do	E&c[171]
12	203	Jones	Olivia	mulatto	25	5' 5"	nas	same	11 June	E&c[172]
12	204	Wood	Nancy	dm^u	c. 38	5' 3½"	nasom	same	18 June	
12	203	Thomas	Sally	dm^u	c. 25	5' 3¼"	a scar in left side of the neck	same	18 June	
12	204	Wood[246]	James	mulatto	19 y	5' 5½"	nasom	same	18 June	
12	205	Toulson [352 -- Warner Weaver]	Henry	dm^u	18 y	5' 8¾" h	a flesh mark on his right arm	same	14 Augt	
12	206	Bell	Ann	m^uw	19 yoa	5' 7½" h	a small mark on her breast	same	15 Augt.	
12	207	Bell	Coleman	bm	57 y	5' 7"	scar on breast & 3 fingers of right[173]	BF	10 Sept	E&cbc[174]
12	208	Bell	Mary	dm^ug	rising 11	4' 4½"	nvmos	BF^N	11 Sept 1827	
12	209	Bell	Dorcas Kelly	same	same	4' 2½"	nmos	same	11 Sept 1827	

[87]201 formerly 83 85 & 97.

[88]Presented her child Ann 8 years of age.

"Northumberland County, Virginia, Register of Free Negroes, 1803-1849."									
PART III: 1821-1830									
P #	Reg. #	Name, Last	Name, First	Colour	Age	Stature	Marks or scars	BF or EMAN	Date of Register	When Certified
12	210[89]	Bee[147]	Vincent	dm[u]	c. 27	5' 7"	deep scar on the left cheek	same	4 March 1828	
12	211	Thomas	Winder	bm[u]	c. 21	5' 9¾" h	nomos	same	11 mar 1828	E&fc[175]
12	212	Gillespie[361]	John	dm[u]	c. 30	5' 10½" h	nmos	same	9 June 1828	E&fc[176]
12	213	Gillespie	Mary	bm[u]	c. 21	5' 4" h	a scar on the shoulder	same	9 June 1828	E&fc[177]
12	214?[M]	Toulson[346, 507]	Maritchia	dm[u]	c. 19	5' 2½" h	a flesh mark under the left ear	same	26 Aug[t] 1828	E&fc[178]
13	215[90]	Toulson[182]	James	mulatto	24 yrs.	5' 10" h	small scar on his right side	BF[N]	12th Nov. 1828	Ebtc[179]
13	216	Rich	Armistead	dm[u]	28	5' 11⅛"h	a lump on the breast[180]	BF[181]	21 Apl 1829	E&fc[182]
13	217	Toulson	Eliza	dm[u]	18	5' 1½" h	namos	BF[N]	11 Apl 1829	Ebtc&fc[183]
13	218	Bell	John	dm[u]	26	5' 8" h	a flesh mark below breast bone[184]	BF[L]	9 May 1829	
13	219	Gillespie	Griffin	mulatto	24 yrs.	5' 10¼"	a scar between the eyes &[185]	BF[N]	11 May 1829	E&fc[186]

[89]210 formerly 147.

[90]215 formerly 182.

"Northumberland County, Virginia, Register of Free Negroes, 1803-1849." PART III: 1821-1830									
P #	Reg. #	Name, Last	Name, First	Colour	Age	Stature	Marks or scars	BF or EMAN	Date of Register	When Certified
13	220	Toulson[442]	Henry	dm[u]	19 yrs.	6' h	a scar in the forehead &[187]	same	12 May 1829	E&fc[188]
13	221	Thomas	Benjamin	dm[u]	21 yrs.	5' 9¾" h	namos	same	13 May 1829	E&fc[189]
13	222	Gaskins	Winny	bm[u]	75 yrs.	5' 4½" h	a scar on the right hand	Eman[190]	8th June 1829	E&fcbtc[191]
13	223	Gaskins	Israel	dm[u]	70	5' 4½" h	namos	same	8th June 1829	Ebtc&fc[192]
13	224	Nicken	Cyrus	black	25	5' 9½" h	a scar on the right arm	BF[N]	8 June 1829	Ebtc&fc[193]
13	225	Day	W[m]	mulatto	26	5' 5¾" h	a scar on the left arm	BF[N]	13 July 1829	
13	226	Pierce	Moses	mulatto	52	5' 6" h	a scar on the right leg	BF[194]	17 July 1829	
13	227	Clarke	Delia	bm[u]	20	5' 4" h	a scar under the chin	BF[N]	8th Aug[t] 1829	Ebtc&fc[195]
13	228	Evans	John H.	mulatto	26	6' & ¾" h	namos	BF[N]	10 Aug[t] 1829	Ebtc&fc[196]
14	229	Nicken	Polly	mulatto	17	5' 5"&½"h	mole over the left eye	BF[N]	10 Aug[t] 1829	Ebtc&fc[197]
14	230	Nicken	Betty	mulatto	15	4' 11" h	namos	same	10 Aug[t] 1829	Ebtc&fc[198]
14	231	Nicken	Nancy	dm[u]	14	5' 1½" h	namos	same	10 Aug[t] 1829	Ebtc&fc[199]

	"Northumberland County, Virginia, Register of Free Negroes, 1803-1849." PART III: 1821-1830

P #	Reg. #	Name, Last	Name, First	Colour	Age	Stature	Marks or scars	BF or EMAN	Date of Register	When Certified
14	232	Nicken	Cath.	bm^u	40	5' 6¾" h	namos	same	10 Augt 1829	Ebtc&fc[200]
14	233	Nicken	Amos	dm^u	66	5' 8½" h	a wen on the back of the neck	same	10 Augt 1829	Ebtc&fc[201]
14	234	Brenn?	Sally (Lilly)	bm^u	25	5' 4½" h	namos	BF	10 Augt 1829	Ebtc&fc[202]
14	235[91]	Bee[147, 210]	Vincent	dm^u	28	5' 7" h	deep scar on the left cheek	BF^N	12 Oct^o 1829	Ebtc&fc[203]
14	236	Bee	Mary	bm^u	20	5' 5" h	namos	BF	12 Oct^o 1829	Ebtc&fc[204]
14	237	Carpenter	Molly	bm^u	22?	5' 7" h	a scar on the left hands	BF^N	12 Oct^o 1829	Ebtc&fc[205]
14	238	Thomas	Hiram	dm^u	22	5' 10" h	a scar on the left rist bone	same	7 Nov. 1829	Ebtc&fc[206]
14	239	Tate	Sally	bm^u	20	5' 7" h	namos	BF^N	11 Jany 1830	Ebtc&fc[207]
14	240	Hurst[566]	John	same	21	5' 3½" h	scar on the right cheek	BF^N	11 Jany 1830	Ebtc&fc[208]
14	241	Keiser	John W.	same	21	5' 11" h	a scar on the breast	BF^N	11 Jany 1830	Ebtc&fc[209]
14	242	Ewell	Renton	same	21	5' 11½" h	a scar on the right rist	same	11 Jany 1830	Ebtc&fc[210]

[91]235 formerly 147.

P #	Reg. #	Name, Last	Name, First	Colour	Age	Stature	Marks or scars	BF or EMAN	Date of Register	When Certified
							"Northumberland County, Virginia, Register of Free Negroes, 1803-1849." PART III: 1821-1830			
15	243	Ewell	Warner	bm[u]	20 y	5' 6" h	namos	BF[N]	11 Jany 1830	Ebc&fc[211]
15	244	Wood	John	m[u]	20	5' 2" h	scar on right thigh a little above knee[212]	same	11 Jany 1830	Ebc&fc[213]
15	245[92]		James[195]	Black	34	5' 7"	scar on left arm	Eman[214]	5 March 1830	Ebc&fc[215]
15	246[93]	Wood[204]	James	bm[u]	22	5' 11"	2 scars on the knee	BF[N]	19 May 1830	Ebc&fc[216]
15	247	Carpenter	Jas.	dm[u]	18	5' 8"	namos	same	17 June 1830	Ebc&fc[217]
15	248	Wood	Walter	bm[u]	21	5' 7" h	a small scar on the neck	same	25 June 1830	Ebc&fc[218]
15	249[94]		Lucy[197]	dw	25	5' h	namos	Eman[219]	10 July 1830	Ebc&fc[220]
15	250	Toulson	Harriet	b[r]w	16	5' 3½" h	a flesh mark on the back of the neck	BF[N]	7 Augt 1830	Ebc&fc[221]
15	251	Bell	James	dm	22	5' 9" h	namos	BF[N]	10 Sept[r] 1830	Ebc&fc[222]
15	252	Bee[338]	Hiram	bm[u]	15	5' ½" h	mark on left shoulder	same	25 Oct[o] 1830	Ebc&fc[223]

[92]245 formerly 195.

[93]246 formerly 204.

[94]249 formerly 197.

"Northumberland County, Virginia, Register of Free Negroes, 1803-1849." PART III: 1821-1830										
P #	Reg. #	Name, Last	Name, First	Colour	Age	Stature	Marks or scars	BF or EMAN	Date of Register	When Certified
15	253	Wood	Brodie	bm[u]	28	5' 6" h	a scar on the right arm	same	4 Nov. 1830	Ebc&fc[224]
15	253	Carpenter	Griffin	dark	30	5' 4"h	a scar on the left shin bone	same	8 Nov 1830	Ebc&fc[225]
15	254[95]	Weaver[45]	Sally	mulatto	56	5' 4" h	thick made a scar on the left arm.	same	13 Dec[r] 1830	Ebc&fc[226]

[95]254 formerly 45.

PART IV: 1831-1840

"Northumberland County, Virginia, Register of Free Negroes, 1803-1849."
PART IV: 1831-1840

P #	Reg. #	Name, Last	Name, First	Colour	Age	Stature	Marks or scars	BF or EMAN	Date of Register	When Certified
[15]	[255]	[missing number]								
[15]	[256]	[Kelly[433]]	[Washington]							
15	257	Day	Ellis	dark	14	4' 9" h	a scar under the left jaw bone	same	28 Feb. 1831	Ebc&fc[227]
16	258	Kelly	Mary	Bright	13	4' 11" h	a scar over the left eye brow	BF[N]	28 Feb. 1831	Ebc&fc[228]
16	259	Day	Ann	dark	12	4' 6" h	namos	same	same	Ebc&fc[229]
16	260	Day	Harriet	dark	10	4' 4" h	the left eye deformed by a burn	same	same	
16	261	Kelly	Nancy	bright	39	5' 7" h	a scar on the right wrist	same	same	Ebc&fc[230]
16	262	Kelly	Joseph	dark	50	5' 8½" h	a scar in the bottom of the right foot.	same	same	Ebc&fc[231]
16	263[96]	Day[137]	Jane	mulatto	56	5' 3" h	a scar on the forehead	same	1st Apl 1831	Ebc&fc[232]
16	264	Causey	Eliza	bright	22	5' 2"	namos	same	4 Apl 1831	Ebc&fc[233]
16	265	Carpenter	Betsy	bright	13	4' 7"	same	same	7 Apl 1831	Ebc&fc[234]
16	266	Carpenter	Tho	bright	9	4' 3"	same	same	7 Apl 1831	Ebtc&fc[235]

[96]263 formerly 137.

				"Northumberland County, Virginia, Register of Free Negroes, 1803-1849."					
				PART IV: 1831-1840					

P #	Reg. #	Name, Last	Name, First	Colour	Age	Stature	Marks or scars	BF or EMAN	Date of Register	When Certified
16	267	Kelley	David H	bright	8	4' 2½" h	same	same	8 April 1831	Ebtc&fc[236]
16	268	Kelley	Joel	bright	7	4' 4" h	same	same	8 Apl 1831	Ebtc&fc[237]
16	269	Carpenter	Nancy	dark	28	5' 3½" h	a scar on the right cheek & left wrist	same	7 May 1831	Ebtc&fc[238]
16	270	Carpenter	Carlos	bright	21	5' 10" h	namos	same	9 May 1831	Ebtc&fc[239]
16	271	Boid	Austin	dark	28	5' 11" h	a scar under the right eye & on right arm.	same	9 May 1831	Ebtc&fc[240]
16	272	Causey	John	bright	18	5' 9"	namos	same	9 May 1831	Ebtc&fc[241]
16	273	Causey	Landon	bright	16	5' 8"	a scar on the right temple	same	9 May 1831	Ebtc&fc[242]
17	274	Carpenter	Robert	bm	26 y	5' 5" h	small scar on the right	BF[N]	13 May 1831	Ebtc&fc[243]
17	275	Bee	Corbin	bright	26	5' 8" h	small scar the right side the neck	same	7 June 1831	Ebtc&fc[244]
17	276	Bee	William	bright	18	6' 2" h	scar over left eye	same	7 June 1831	Ebtc&fc[245]
17	277	Laws	Daniel	bright	34	5' 6" h	namos	same	22 June 1831	

44

P #	Reg. #	Name, Last	Name, First	Colour	Age	Stature	Marks or scars	BF or EMAN	Date of Register	When Certified
							"Northumberland County, Virginia, Register of Free Negroes, 1803-1849." PART IV: 1831-1840			
17	278	Laws	Nancy	bright	25	4' 10" h	small scar the back of the right hand	same	3ᵈ July 1831	Ebtc&fc[246]
17	279	Thomas	Washington	dark	22	5' 7" h	small scar the left arm	same	18 July 1831	Ebtc&fc[247]
17	280	Haw	Peter	bʳm	48	5' 3" h	npmos	same	4 Aug 1831	
17	281	Thompson	Henry	bm	32	5' 6" h	a scar from burn on the right arm	same	11 Aug. 1831	
17	282	Sank	Rachel	bʳw	20	5' 4" h	a scar over the left eye n the left wrist	same	10 Octᵒ 1831	
17	283	Toulson	Eliza	dw	25	5' 5½" h	a scar on the left cheek bone	same	17 Octᵒ 1831	Ebtc&fc[248]
17	284	Watkins	Patty	bʳw	27	5' 4" h	flesh mark on the nose	same	17 Octᵒ 1831	
17	285	Ewell	Warner	bʳm	21	5' 7" h	a scar on the right leg	same	14 Nov 1831	Ebtc&fc[249]
17	287	Elliston	Betsy	bʳw	27	5' 3"	namos	same	15 Nov. 1831	Ebtc&fc[250]
17	288	Walker	John	same	40	5' 4"	a scar on the nose & upper lip	same	15 Nov 1831	
17	289	Burke	Ellen	bw	28	5' 4"	a scar on the left cheek bone	BF	13 Decʳ 1831	Ebtc&fc[251]

"Northumberland County, Virginia, Register of Free Negroes, 1803-1849." PART IV: 1831-1840									
P #	Reg. #	Name, Last	Name, First	Colour	Age	Stature	Marks or scars	BF or EMAN	Date of Register	When Certified
18	290	Walker	Monroe	bᵣm do.	17 y ~~21~~	5' 7" h	a scar on the left breast & right leg	BFᴺ	2ᵈ Mar. 1832	Ebtc&fc
18	291	Armstead	Addison	lm	21	5' 6½" h	a scar on the back of the right hand	same	12 " "	Ebtc&fc[252]
18	292	Casty[468]	Peter	dm	22	4' 11½" h	burn on right wrist & scar on left temple[253]	same	12 " "	Ebtc&fc[254]
18	293	Casty	James	dm	21	5' 6¼" h	scar in the forehead	same	12	Ebtc&fc[255]
18	294	Spriddle	John	l do	21	5' 8" h	dark dimple on chin &scar in the right knee[256]	same	12	Ebtc&fc[257]
18	295	Casty	John	dm	24	5' 2" h	a scar on the right wrist and left knee	same	13	Ebtc&fc[258]
18	296	Corsey	Wᵐ	bᵣb	16	4' 11½" h	a broken arm	same	9 April	Ebtc&fc[259]
18	297	Anderson	Grates	bᵣm	21`	5' 7" h	scar near the left eye & on ~~right~~ left arm.	Same	14 May	Ebtc&fc[260]
18	298	Sutton	Moses	bm	26	5' 4" h	a scar below the instep of right foot	Eman[261]	14 May	Ebtc&fc[262]
18	299	Bee	Walter	db	6	3' 10"	nsom	BFᴺ	4 June	
18	300	Bee	Sally	bᵣg	5	3' 4"	cross-eyed with a burn on the right cheek	same	4 June	
18	301	Bee	Betty	dg	3	2' 7"	nvmos	same	4 June	Ebtc&fc[263]

*		"Northumberland County, Virginia, Register of Free Negroes, 1803-1849." PART IV: 1831-1840							

P #	Reg. #	Name, Last	Name, First	Colour	Age	Stature	Marks or scars	BF or EMAN	Date of Register	When Certified
18	302	Jordan	John	b^{r}m	21	5' 14" h	a scar on the upper lip & right side	BF[264]	11 June	
18	303	Weaver	Jno. B	dm	28	5' 8" h	a scar in the forehead & on left arm	BF^N	11 June	
18	304	Toulson	Sally	b^{r}w	46	5' 5"	namos	same	11 June	
19	[305]	Weaver	?rner	?m	22	5' 5"	namos	Bf^N	June 11 1832	E&fc[265]
19	[306]	Wood	W^m	b^{r}m	21	5' 5"	a scar on the right hand	same	June 11 1832	Ebtc&fc[266]
19	307	Thomas	Winder	b^{r}m		5' 9¾"	a scar on the left leg	same	June 11 1832	
19	308	Wadkins	Lucretia	b^{r}w	21	5' 10¼"	a scar on the right arm	same	July 9 1832	E&fc[267]
19	309	Bee	Ansie	dw		5' "	a scar on the left arm	same	July 9 1832	Ebtc&fc[268]
19	310	Peters	John	b^{r}m	43	5' 7½" h	scar on left side of head & breast	same	Sep. 10 1832	
19	311	Nicken	Cath	b^{r}w	46	5' 7½" h	namos	same	7 Nov. 1832	
19	312	Grain	James	b^{r}m	20	5' 6"	namos	same	11 Mar. 1833	E&fc[269]
19	313	Nicken	Cyrus	dm	27	5' 10½" h	2 scars on the forehead	same	9 Dec. 1833	E&fc[270]

P #	Reg. #	Name, Last	Name, First	Colour	Age	Stature	Marks or scars	BF or EMAN	Date of Register	When Certified
							"Northumberland County, Virginia, Register of Free Negroes, 1803-1849." PART IV: 1831-1840			
19	314	Nicken	Peter	dm	22	5' 4" h	scars forehead & left side chin bone[271]	same	9 Dec 1833	
19	[315]	Sank	Rachel	b^{r}w	23	5' 4"	a scar over the left eye & on left wrist	same	12 May 1834	E&fc[272]
19	[316]	Toulson	Martchia	dw	20	5' 1"	a scar on the forehead	same	12 May 1834	E&ftbc[273]
19	[317]	~~Weaver~~ Bell	John	dm	30	5' 8½"	scar forehead flesh mark right arm.[274]	same	13 Oct^o 1834	E&ftb[275]
19	[318]	~~Weaver~~ Toulson	Eliza Ann	b^{r}w	31	5' 2"	a scar on the right arm	same	13 Oct^o 1834	E&ftb[276]
19	[319]	Toulson	?^{M}y Ann	dg	15	5' ½"	a scar between upper lip & right cheek	same	13 Oct. 1834	E&ftb[277]
20	[320]	Toulson	Nancy	b^{r}w	27	5' 10" h	nmos	BF^N	July 9 1835	
20	321	Bell	Mary	b^{r}w	18	5' 3"h	nmos	same	July 9. 1835	
20	322	Carpenter	Molly	b^{r}w	54	5' 5" h	a scar on the back of left hand	same	July 9. 1835	
20	323	Carpenter	Griffin	b^{r}m	30	5' 4" h	a scar on the left shin bone	same	July 9. 1835	
20	324	Spriddle	Delia	dw	17	5' 6" h	a scar on the right cheek bone	same	July 9. 1835	

48

	**"Northumberland County, Virginia, Register of Free Negroes, 1803-1849."** **PART IV: 1831-1840**
P #	Reg. #	Name, Last	Name, First	Colour	Age	Stature	Marks or scars	BF or EMAN	Date of Register	When Certified
20	325	Carpenter	Betsy	b^{r}g	16	5' 2" h	nmos	same	July 9 1835	
20	326	Carpenter	Mary	b^{r}g	10	3' 8" h	nmos	same	9 July 1835	
20	327	Carpenter	Hiram	db	3	2' 9" h	nmos	same	9 July 1835	
20	328	Bee	Walter	b^{r}b	11	4' 5"	nmos	same	9 Nov 1835	E&fc[278]
20	329	Day	Hiram	b^{r}m	24	5' 7" h	two scars near the right eye	same	11 Jany 1836	E&fc[279]
20	330	Thomas	Polly	dw	21	5' 2½" h	nmos	same	5th Feb. 1836	E&fc[280]
20	331	Hubbard	Solomon N.	bm	33	5' 2" h	2 scars on the left side of face,[281]	BF^W	8 Feb. 1836	E&fc[282]
20	332	Nickens	Peter	bm	23	5' 4" h	3 scars forehead & one left cheek.[283]	BF^L	11 April 1836	E&fc[284]
20	333	Mason	Fanny	b^{r}w	21	5' 3" h	nvmos	same	9 Sepr 1836	
20	334	Spriddle	Tho.	dm	28	5' 5"	same	same	13 Mar. 1837	E&fc[285]
20	335	Casity	Tho.	b^{r}m	23	5' 11" h	a flesh mark on the right wrist[286]	BF^N	27 May 1837	E&fc[287]

P #	Reg. #	Name, Last	Name, First	Colour	Age	Stature	Marks or scars	BF or EMAN	Date of Register	When Certified
							"Northumberland County, Virginia, Register of Free Negroes, 1803-1849." **PART IV: 1831-1840**			
21	336	Ticer	John	b^{r}m	19	5' 5" h	a scar on the back of the right hand	BF^N	Feb. 20 1838	Ebtc&fc[288]
21	337	Walker	Monroe	b^{r}m	23	5' 8½" h	scar left breast occasioned by burn[289]	BF^N	Aug 12th 1839[290]	Ebtc&fc[291]
21	338[97]	Bee[252]	Hiram	b^{r}m	23	5' ½" h	scar left shoulder & across foot[292]	same	Aug ^{12} 1839	Ebtc&fc[293]
21	339	Robinson	Louisa	b^{r}w	26	5' 2½" h	nmos	same	Augt 12 1839	Ebtc&fc[294]
21	340	Bell	Jane	dg	14	4' 5" h	nmos	BF^L	Augt 20 1839	
21	341	Bell	Sally	b^{r}g	12	4' 4" H	a scar on the head	same	Augt 20 1839	
21	342	James	Sally Ann	b^{r}g	11	4' 5½"	right arm deformed	same	9th Sep. 1839	
21	343	Thomas	Nancy	b^{r}w	45	5' 3" h	namos	same[295]	same	Ebtc&fc[296]
21	344	Thomas	Ann	b^{r}g	13	4' 5"	right hand scared	same	same	Ebtc&fc[297]
21	345	Cornish	Juliet	b^{r}g	17	5' 4"	nvmos	same	same	Ebtc&fc[298]
21	346[98]	Toulson [214, 507]	Maritchia	dw	25	5' 3"	a scar on her forehead	same	same	Ebtc&fc[299]

---

[97] 338 formerly 252.

[98] 346 formerly 214.

\multicolumn{10}{c}{**"Northumberland County, Virginia, Register of Free Negroes, 1803-1849."** **PART IV: 1831-1840**}									
P #	Reg. #	Name, Last	Name, First	Colour	Age	Stature	Marks or scars	BF or EMAN	Date of Register	When Certified
21	347	Lewis	Warner	bm	23	5' 10" h	scar on right arm occasioned by a burn[300]	same	10 Oct° 1839	Ebtc&fc[301]
21	348	Thomas	Jno.	b^rm	21	5' 5½" h	scar on lesser toe & top right foot[302]	same	14 Oct. 1839	Ebtc&fc[303]
21	349	Weaver	Tho D	b^rm	23	5' 8"	nmos	same	11 Nov. 1839	Ebtc&fc[304]
22	350	Weaver	W^m	b^rm	25	5' 10½" h	nmos	BF^N	1839. Nov. 11	Ebtc&fc[305]
22	351	Weaver	Elizabeth	b^rw	21	5' 4½" h	nmos	same	same	E&fc[306]
22	352[99]	Weaver [205 -- Henry Toulson]	Warner	b^rm	27	5' 6" h	nmos	same	same	E&fc[307]
22	353	Wood	Hiram	b^rm	17	5' 8" h	nmos	same	1840 Feb 10	E&fc[308]
22	354	Sorrell	Jas	b^rm	25	5' 5½"	2 scars on the back of the left hand	same	same	E&fc[309]
22	355	Thomas	Jas.	b^rm	19	5' 6"	nmos	same	same	E&fc[310]
22	356	Sorrell	Henry	b^rm	22	5' 8"	nmos	same	same	E&fc[311]
22	357	Sorrell	Walter	b^rm	19	5' 9"	a scar above the nose	same	1840 Feb. 14	
22	358	Opie	Daniel	b^rm	24	5' 5" h	nvmos	same	1840 Mar. 9	E&fc[312]

[99]352 formerly 205.

	"Northumberland County, Virginia, Register of Free Negroes, 1803-1849." PART IV: 1831-1840								

P #	Reg. #	Name, Last	Name, First	Colour	Age	Stature	Marks or scars	BF or EMAN	Date of Register	When Certified
22	359	Thomas	John	dm	25	5' 8" h	a scar on the right thumb	same	1840 Mar. 9	E&fc[313]
22	360	Bell	Elizabeth	b'w	19	5' 5" h	nvmos	same	1840 Mar. 12	E&fc[314]
22	361[100]	Gillespie [212]	John	dm	39	5' 4½" h	nrs	same	1840 April 13	E&fc[315]
23	362	Day	Juliet Ann	b'w	24	5' 3" h	a scar below the right cheek bone	BF[N]	June 8. 1840	E&fc[316]
23	363	Weaver	Celia Ann	b'w	15	5' 4" h	a scar on the right elbow	same	same	
23	364	Owings	Lavala	b'w	18	5' 3" h	nvmos	same	same	E&fc[317]
23	365	Credit	Tho	b'm	40	5' 7"	nmos	same	July 13 1840	E&fc[318]
23	366	Credit	Eliza	b'w	20	5' 1" h	a scar on the right thumb	same	same	E&fc[319]
23	367	Thomas	Polly	b'w	16	5'	nvmos	same	same	E&fc[320]
23	368	Casty	John	dm	32	5' 2"	a scar on the right wrist & left knee	same		
23	369	Sank	Hannah	dw	26	5' 3"	a scar on the back of the right hand	same	14 Sept 1840	E&fc[321]

[100]361 formerly 212.

PART V: 1841-1849

"Northumberland County, Virginia, Register of Free Negroes, 1803-1849."
PART V: 1841-1849

P #	Reg. #	Name, Last	Name, First	Colour	Age	Stature	Marks or scars	BF or EMAN	Date of Register	When Certified
23	370	Wood	Hiram	b^rm	18	5' 8" h	nvmos	same	11 Jany 1841	E&fc[322]
23	371	Credit	Bush	b^rm	21	5' 6"h	a mashed finger on the right hand	same	same	E&fc[323]
23	372	Ticer	Harriet	b^rw	21	5' 3" h	nvmos	same	8 Feb. 1841	E&fc[324]
23	373	Jones	Armstead	same	42	5' 8" h	scar on the right cheek bone	same	5 Mar. 1841	E&fc[325]
23	374	Sank	John Jr.	dm	32	5' 5"	nmos	same	8 March 1841	E&fc[326]
23	375	Ticer	Gilbert	dm	21	5' 7" h	nvmos	same	12 July 1841	E&fc[327]
24	376	Day	Harriet	dark	21	5' 5" h	left eye effected & flesh mark upon breast	BF^N	Augt 9 1841	E&fc[328]
24	377	Toulson	Sally	b^rw	50	5' 5"	nvmos	same	9 Nov. 1841	
24	378	Wood	Walter	b^rb	17	5' 1" h	a scar on the back of the right hand	same	10 Jany 1842	E&fc[329]
24	379	Weaver	Henry	b^rb	18	5' 1½" h	a small scar on the left hand	same	14 Feb 1842	E&fc[330]
24	380	Credit	Tho	b^rb	15	5' ½"	nmos	same	same	
24	381	Casity	Ann	b^rw	20	5' 4½" h	a scar over the left eye	same	14 Mar 1842	
24	382	Casity	Delia	b^rw	25	5' 4"	nvmos	same	11 April 1842	E&fc[331]

54

P #	Reg. #	Name, Last	Name, First	Colour	Age	Stature	Marks or scars	BF or EMAN	Date of Register	When Certified
24	383	Weaver	Ann	b^rw	22	5' 3"	a scar on the right thumb	same	9 May 1842	
24	384	Blundon	Alice	dw	45	5' 2¾"	nvmos	same	9 May 1842	E&fc[332]
24	385	Weaver	Jno	dm	21	5' 6" h	nvmos	same	13 June 1842	
24	386	Bee	Uriar	b^rm	22	5' 10" h	a scar above the left eye brow	same	11 July 1842	E&fc[333]
24	387	Laws	Baldwin	dm	23	5' 8½" h	a flesh mark on the forehead	same	11 July 1842	E&fc[334]
24	388	Bird	James	dm	20	5' 9" h	a scar upon the upper lip	same	10 Oct° 1842	E&fc[335]
24	389	Obear	James	b^rm	21	5' 8½" h	nvmos	same	10 Oct° 1842	E&fc[336]
26	399	Spriddle	Martin	bright	22	5' 9"	flesh mark on the left cheek	BF^N	14 Nov 1842	E&fc[337]
26	400	Sank	Spencer	bright	22	5' 9½" h	nvmos	same	10 Feb 1843	E&fc[338]
26	401	Sorrell	Edward	bright	21	5' 9"	scar back right hand & under lip[339]	same	13 Feb. 1843	E&fc[340]
26	402	Sorrell	Steptoe	bright	21	5' 6"	a scar between the eyebrows	same	13 Feb 1843	E&fc[341]
26	403	Martin	Jno	bright	22	5' 10"	nmos	same	13 Feb 1843	E&fc[342]

"Northumberland County, Virginia, Register of Free Negroes, 1803-1849."
PART V: 1841-1849

"Northumberland County, Virginia, Register of Free Negroes, 1803-1849."
PART V: 1841-1849

P #	Reg. #	Name, Last	Name, First	Colour	Age	Stature	Marks or scars	BF or EMAN	Date of Register	When Certified
26	404	Sorrell	Walter	bright	22	5' 10"	a scar lt. eyebrow & rt. thumb[343]	same	13 Feb 1843	E&fc[344]
26	405	Nicken	Robert	bright	18	5' 6"	a scar in the forehead	same	13 Feb. 1843	E&fc[345]
26	406	Credit	Tho.	bright	16	5' 3"	nvmos	same	13 Feb 1843	E&fc[346]
26	407	Bell	Coleman	black	73	5' 6" h	scars on breast & 3 fingers of right hand injured	BF	28 April 1843	E&fc[347]
26	408	Sorrell	Richard	bright	26	5' 10" h	a scar on the left cheek bone & inside left hand	same	8 May 1843	E&fc[348]
26	409	Jones	Wm	dark	22	5' 7" h	a scar over the right eyebrow	same	8 May 1843	E&fc[349]
26	410	Boyd	Thomas	bright	29	5' 7" h	nvmos	same	12 June 1843	
27	411	Sank	Ann	bright	23	5' 2" h	nvmos	BF[N]	13 Nov 1843	E&fc[350]
27	412	Wood	Margaret	bright	21	5' 3"	same	same	same	E&fc[351]
27	413	Sorrell	Elizabeth	bright	23	5' 3"	same	same	same	E&fc[352]
27	414	Thomas	Luky	bright	4	5'	same	same	same	E&fc[353]
27	415	Spriddle	Jesse	bright	43	5' 5"	same	same	same	E&fc[354]
27	416	Spriddle	Mary	bright	25	5' 5½"	a flesh mole over left eye	same	same	E&fc[355]
27	417	Edmonds	Juliet Ann	bright	8	3' 8"	nmos			E&fc[356]
27	418	Spriddle	Hiliary	bright	17	5' 1"	same	same	same	E&fc[357]

"Northumberland County, Virginia, Register of Free Negroes, 1803-1849."
PART V: 1841-1849

P #	Reg. #	Name, Last	Name, First	Colour	Age	Stature	Marks or scars	BF or EMAN	Date of Register	When Certified
27	419	Sorrell	Jno.	bright	17	5' 5"	a scar on the left hand	same	same	E&fc[358]
27	420	Spriddle	Lucy	bright	20	4' 11"	a scar on the left wrist	same	same	E&fc[359]
27	421	Thomas	Sophia	bright	23	4' 11"	nmos	same	same	E&fc[360]
27	422	Sorrell	Darky [Dorcas]	bright	52	5' 5½"	a flesh mole on left cheek	same	same	E&fc[361]
27	423	Credit	Sally	dark	49	5' 6"	a scar on the left thumb	same	same	E&fc[362]
28	424	Weaver	Joseph	bright	55	5' 7½" h	left eye injured	BF[N]	11 Dec. 1843	E&fc[363]
28	425	Carpenter	Bertha	bright	19	5' 11½" h	a scar over the left eye	same	8 Jany 1844	E&fc[364]
28	426	Bell	Jane	dark	18	4' 10"	nmos	same	12 Jany 1844	
28	427	Bell	Sally	bright	14	5' 6"	nmos	same	same	
28	428	Sorrell	Henderson	bright	15	5'	nvmos	same	12 March	E&fc[365]
28	429	Thomas	Henry	bright	23	6' 1"	nmos	same	same	E&fc[366]
28	430	Keizer	Robert	bright	23	5' 6"	nmos	same	same	
28	431	Laws	Robert	bright	24	5' 7"	nmos	same	13th May	E&fc[367]
28	432	Jones	Alfred	black	20	5' 3"	a scar in the forehead	same	13 May	E&fc[368]
28	433[101]	Kelly[256]	Washington	dark	28	5' 1½"	a scar on forehead area	same	13 May	E&fc[369]
28	434	Laws	Austin	dark	22	5' 3"	a scar on the right cheek	same	13 May	E&fc[370]

[101]433 formerly 256.

P #	Reg. #	Name, Last	Name, First	Colour	Age	Stature	Marks or scars	BF or EMAN	Date of Register	When Certified
							"Northumberland County, Virginia, Register of Free Negroes, 1803-1849." PART V: 1841-1849			
28	435	Laws	Daniel	bright	46	5' 6" h	a scar on the right eyebrow	same	10 June "	E&fc[371]
28	436	Bee	Walter	bright	19	5' 9"	nvmos	same	8 Jul	
28	437		Eliza	dark	21	5' 2" h	a scar on the left wrist	Eman[372]	July 8	E&fc[373]
28	438	Thomas	Harriet	dark	28	5' 5" h	scar on the back of the right hand	BF[N]	9 Sept "	E&fc[374]
29	439	Bee	Austin	bright	30	5' 6" h	?	BF[N]	1844 Sept 9	E&fc[375]
29	440	Blueford	W[m]	bright	25	6' 2"	nvmos	same	same	E&fc[376]
29	441	Bee	Sarah	bright	17	5' 1" h	a scar on the right cheek & crosseyed	same	7 Nov. 1844	E&fc[377]
29	442[102]	Toulson[220]	Henry	bright	30	5' 11" h	a scar in the forehead & right arm	same	7 Dec.	
29	443	Drake	Addison	bright	30	5' 10" h	a scar on the left wrist	BF[378]	9 Dec 1844	E&fc[379]
29	444	Toulson	Archibald	bright	18	5' 12" h	two scars on the left leg	BF[N]	10 Feb 1845	E&fc[380]
29	445	Sank	Winder	black	19	5' 5" h	a scar on the right wrist & right leg	same	same	E&fc[381]
29	446	Sorrell	Washington	dark	21	5' 6" h	a scar near the left eye & on the right wrist	same	11 Mar. 1845	E&fc[382]
29	447	Moore[718]	Daniel	bright	31	5' 8" h	nvmos	same	9 June 1845	E&fc[383]

[102]442 formerly 220.

	"Northumberland County, Virginia, Register of Free Negroes, 1803-1849." PART V: 1841-1849

P #	Reg. #	Name, Last	Name, First	Colour	Age	Stature	Marks or scars	BF or EMAN	Date of Register	When Certified
29	448	Casity	Ann	bright	23	5' 5" h	a scar above the left eye	same	9 June 1845	E&fc[384]
29	449	Lewis	James	bright	18	5' 8" h	a scar over the right eye	same	9 June 1845	E&fc[385]
	450	[missing number]								
30	451	Laws[723]	Robert	b[r]m	25 yoa	5' 7" h	nmosv	BF[N]	15 July 1845	
30	452	Bee	Harriet	b[r]w	18	5' 5" h	a cut thumb on the right hand	same	5 Augt 1845	E&fc
30	453	Bee	Ann	b[r]w	29	5' 5" h	a scar over the right eye	same	5 Augt 1845	
30	454	Coats	Levina	b[r]w	40	5' 4"	a scar on the right ear	same	8th Sep 1845	E&fc
30	455	Sank	Charlotte	b[r]w	30	5' 4" h	nmos	same	10 Nov 1845	E&fc
30	456	Sank	John	b[r]m	35	5' 8" h	a scar on forehead	same	10 Nov. 1845	E&fc
30	457	Sorrell	Darius	b[r]m	21	5' 7"	a scar on the forehead	same	9 Feb 1846	E&fc
30	458	Sank	Carlos	dark	18	5' 2"	a scar over the left eye	same	9 Feb 1846	E&fc
30	459	Sank	James	bright	18	5' 8"	a scar on the right temple	same	9 Feb 1846	E&fc
30	460	Sank	Nancy	bright	18	5' 2"	a scar on the left wrist	same	9 Feb 1846	E&fc

P #	Reg. #	Name, Last	Name, First	Colour	Age	Stature	Marks or scars	BF or EMAN	Date of Register	When Certified
							"Northumberland County, Virginia, Register of Free Negroes, 1803-1849." PART V: 1841-1849			
30	461	Carpenter	Ben	black	46	5' 8"	a scar on the left wrist	same	9 Mar 1846	E&fc
30	462	Carpenter	Eliz.	bright	27	5' 1" h	nmos	same	same	E&fc
30	463	Thomas	Lucretia	dark	17	5' 2" h	a scar on each lesser finger	same	same	E&fc
30	464	Thomas	Mary Ann	bright	19	5' 4"	a scar on the little finger & left eyebrow	same	same	E&fc
30	465	Jones	James	black	19	5' 4"	a scar on the left leg	same	same	E&fc
31	466	Thornton	James	bright	13	4' 6½" h	a scar on the right temple	BF[N]	20 Mar 1846	
31	467	Carpenter	Hiram	dark	13	4' 7½" h	nvmos	same	20 Mar 1846	
31	468[103]	Casity[292]	Peter	dark	36	4' 11½" h	burn on right wrist & scar on teft temple & lip.[386]	same	8 June 1846	E&fc
31	469	Weaver	Mary	dark	21	5' h	a scar over the left eye brow	same	13 July 1846	E&fc
31	470	Bee	A scar	dark	12	4' 10"	a small scar on the forehead & right cheek	same	13 July 1846	
31	471	Spriddle	Thomas	dark	30	5' 6"	nvmos	same	9th Novber 1846	
31	472	Spriddle	Elizabeth	dark	37	5' 4"	nvmos	same	same	
31	473	Spriddle	Thomas Jr.	Dark	14	5'	nvmos	same	same	

[103]468 formerly 292.

"Northumberland County, Virginia, Register of Free Negroes, 1803-1849."
PART V: 1841-1849

P #	Reg. #	Name, Last	Name, First	Colour	Age	Stature	Marks or scars	BF or EMAN	Date of Register	When Certified
31	474	Spriddle	Jane E.	Dark	13	4' 10"	nvmos	same	same	
31	475	Spriddle	Jesse	dark	10	4' 4"	nvmos	same	same	
31	476	Wood	Susan	bright	20	5' 3"	nvmos	BF^N	8th February 1847	1847 February 8th
32	477	Sorrell	Eliza	bright	21	5' 2"	nvmos	BF^N	8th February 1847	1847 8th February
32	478	Sorrell	Judy	bright	19	5' 2"	a scar on right arm	BF^N	8th Feb 1847	1847 8th February
32	479	Causey	William	dark	22	5' 2"	nvmos	BF^N	8th Feby 1847	1847 8th February
32	480	Sank	Robert	bright	18	5' 4"	nvmos	BF^N	8th Feby 1847	1847 8th Febuay
32	481	Boyd	Baldwin	dark	25	5' 3"	nvmos	BF^N	8th Feb 1847	1847 8th Febuay
32	482	Sorrell	Steptoe	bright	24	5' 4"	a scar above the nose	BF^N	8th Febuay 1847	1847 8th Febuay
32	483	Sorrell	William	dark	31	6'	a scar on the left hand	BF^N	8th Febuay 1847	1847 8th Febuay
32	484	Spriddle	James	dark	15	5' 2"	nvmos	BF^N	8th Febuay 1847	

P #	Reg. #	Name, Last	Name, First	Colour	Age	Stature	Marks or scars	BF or EMAN	Date of Register	When Certified
							"Northumberland County, Virginia, Register of Free Negroes, 1803-1849." **PART V: 1841-1849**				
32	485	Nickens	Jane	bright	21	5' 8"	nvmos	BF[N]	8th March 1847	1847 March 8th
32	486	Keiser	Catherine	bright	22	5' 6"	scar on the left side of her head	BF[N]	9th March 1847	March 9th[387]
32	487	Cornish	Hiram	bright	26	5' 10"	scar on the left arm, right leg and right foot.	BF[N]		
32	488	Jones	Alfred	black	21	5' 4" h	scar over the left eye	BF[N]	12th April 1847	April 12th[388]
32	489	Jones	Nancy	black	35	4' 4"	scar on the left arm	BF[N]	14 Jun --	June 14th[389]
32	490	Boyd	Eliza	bright	25	5' 2"	scar on the left leg	BF[N]	14th Jn 1847	1847 June
33	491	Weaver	Lucy	bright	37	5'	cataract	BF[N]	16 July 1847	9th August
33	492	Weaver	Ann Maria	bright	7	3' 11"		BF[N]	16 July 1847	9th Aug[390]
33	493	Weaver	Hinton	bright	10 m	2' h		BF[N]	16 July 1847	9th Aug[391]
33	494	Bee	Walter	bright				BF[N]	29 July 1847	
33	495	Weaver	Whittendon	bright	10	4' 3"		BF[N]	23rd August[392]	
33	496	Spriddle	Mottrom	bright	30	5' 5"	scar on his right leg	BF[N]	8 Novr 1847	

"Northumberland County, Virginia, Register of Free Negroes, 1803-1849."
PART V: 1841-1849

P #	Reg. #	Name, Last	Name, First	Colour	Age	Stature	Marks or scars	BF or EMAN	Date of Register	When Certified
33	497	Spriddle	Jane	bright	19	5' 3"	nvnms	BFN	8 Novr 1847	
33	498	Bee	Robert	bright	20-10	5' 10" h	a scar on his forehead & left leg	BFN	14th Feb 1848[393]	14 Feb 1848[394]
33	499	Sorrell	Elizabeth	bright	25	5'	a scar on her neck & finger	BFN	13 Feb 1848[395]	
33	500	Credit	Polly	bright	23	4' 11"	nvnm			
33	501	Bee	Harriet	bright	34	5' 4" h	scar in the back of the neck	BFN	8th May 1848	
34	[501]	Bee	Beverly	dark	14	4' 5"	no mark	BFN		
34	502	Sorrell	Wm	dark	21	5' 11"	no mark	BFN	12 May 1849	
34	503	Bee	Lucy	dark	20	5' 3½"	mark in left sider forehead	BFN	14th April 1849	
34	504	Kent	Henry	dark	23	5' 10" h	mark on his right arm & wt on limb	BFN	May 9 1849	
34	505	Kelly	Ludwell	bright	20	5' 8" h	scar on his chin & right ankle	BFN	13 Aug 1849[396]	Exfd
34	506	Sank Weaver	Celia Ann	bright	22	5' 5" h	scar on right arm, one in mouth/oneforefiner	BFN	9 Sep	Sept 1849[397]
34	507	Toulson[346, 214]	Marthicia	dark	35	5' 3" h	scar on forehead	BFN		9th Sept 1849
34	508	Thomas	Solomon	dark	35	5' 10"	scar on right wrist			

Northumberland County, Virginia Register of Free Negroes 1849-1858

Key:

General

? = handwriting illegible
First and Last Names are not separated in the original
Blank cells are blank on the original.

Column Headers

P# = Page Number
Reg. # = Number on the Register
Ht. = Height (height is spelled out in the original)
BF or Eman = Born Free or Emancipated
When Cert. = When Certified by the Court

Age

yr = year(s), m = months,
IITA = Infant in the Arms

Height

' = feet
" = inches

Marks or Scars

nvmos = no visible marks or scars
nsom = no scar or mark
nmos = no mark or scar

Born Free or Emancipated

BoD = Born of Ditto
Do = Ditto
BF^L = Born of Free Parents in Lancaster County
BF^N = Born of Free Parents in Northumberland County

Date of Register/When Certified

E&ftbc = Examined & Found to be correct
Feb = February
Aug = August
Sept = September
Oct = October
Octr = October

"Northumberland County, Virginia Register of Free Negroes 1849-1858."

P #	Reg. #	Name, Last	Name, First	Age	Color	Ht.	Marks or scars	BF or Eman	Date of Register	When Cert.
1	508	Toulson	Eliza	17 yr	Dark	5' 2"	nvmos	BFN	8th Oct 1849	
1	509	Sorrell	McCartney	21 yr	bright	5' 4"	scar on forehead & left cheek	BoD	11th Feb 1850	
1	510	Dunaway	Betsey	19 (17)	bright	5' 11"	nvmos	BoD	8th April 1850	
1	511	Sorrell	Judith	23 yr	bright	5' 6"	nvmos	BoD	8th April 1850	
1	512	Johnson	Elizabeth	19 yr	bright	5' 3"	nvmos	BoD	12th Aug 1850	
1	513	Johnson	Polly	16 yr	Dark	4' 11"	scar on the neck	BoD	"	
1	514	Johnson	James	13 yr	Dark	4'	nvmos	BoD	"	
1	515	Jones	Alfred	23 yr	Dark	5' 3"	scar on his forehead	BoD	"	
1	516	Thomas	Solomon	36 yr	Dark	5' 18"	scar on right wrist	BF	8 Sept 1850	
2	517	Thomas	Robert	22	dark	5' 9"	scar on left cheek & wrist	BF		
2	518	Thomas	Sukey	50	dark	5' 6"	scar right arm & left wrist	BFN		
2	519	Thomas	Judy Anne	35	dark	5' 3"	scar under eye & in nose	BF		
2	520	Bradger	Elizabeth	13	bright	4' 11"	scar on breast	BF		

P #	Reg. #	Name, Last	Name, First	Age	Color	Ht.	Marks or scars	BF or Eman	Date of Register	When Cert.
2	521	Thomas	Jane	13	bright	5' 4"	scar on right hand	BF		
2	522	Thomas	Sadie	12	bright	5' 4½"	scar on right hand	BF		
2	523	Thomas	Lucy	24	bright	5' 2"	scar on left shoulder	BF		
3	524	Ticer	Robert	25	bright	5' 10"	nvmos	BF[N]		
3	525	Weaver	Maurice	20	bright	5' 11"	nvmos	BoD		
3	526	Blundon	James	19	dark	5' 9"	scar over right eye	BoD		
3	527	Ticer	Winder	16	bright	6'	nvmos	BoD		
3	528	Bee	Walter	24	bright	6'	nvmos	BoD		
3	529	Sorrell	Elizabeth	25	bright	5' 2"	scar on left hand	BoD		
3	530	Martin	Carmez	21	bright	5'	no scars	BoD		
3	531	Carpenter	May	23	bright	5' 2"	scar over eyebrow & under chin	BoD		
4	532	Thomas	Hiram	22	bright	6' 1"	scar on right hand & on belly	BF		
4	533	Toulson	Jas	28	bright	6'	scar right eyebrow & right hand	BoD		
4	534	Causey	Jas	17	bright	5' 7"	scar on forehead	BoD		
4	535	Causey	Jn.	21	bright	5' 8"	no scar	BoD		
4	536	Spriddle	Tempest	37	dark	5' 6"	nvmos	BoD		
4	537	Spriddle	Lucy	7	bright	5' 6"	no scar	BoD		
4	538	Casity	Mary	15	dark	5' 1"	no scar	BoD		

"Northumberland County, Virginia Register of Free Negroes 1849-1858."

66

P #	Reg. #	Name, Last	Name, First	Age	Color	Ht.	Marks or scars	BF or Eman	Date of Register	When Cert.
							"Northumberland County, Virginia Register of Free Negroes 1849-1858."			
5	539	Jones	Mariah	15	dark	4' 11"	scar on left foot	BF		
5	540	Boyd	Eliza	30	bright	5' 3"	scar on forehead	BoD		
5	541	Casity	Maranda	25	dark	4' 11"	scar on ankle	BoD		
5	542	Casity	Elizabeth	40	dark	5'	shot in right arm	BoD		
5	543	Casity	Sarah	20	dark	5'	scar on right cheek	BoD		
5	544	Ticer	Eliza	23	dark	5'	scar on forehead	BoD		
5	545	Thomas	Sarah	17	bright	5' 8"	no scar	BoD		
6	546	Spriddle	Robt	14	bright	4' 8"	scar on right leg	BF		
6	547	Thomas	Wm	25	dark	6'	no scar	BoD		
6	548	Toulson	Henry							
6	549	Causey	Holland C.	48	bright	5' 8"	scar on right had	BoD		
6	550	Causey	Betsy	36	bright	5' 6"	no scar	BoD		
6	551	Causey	Landon	13	bright	4' 8"	no scar	BoD		
6	552	Sorrell	Washington	26	dark	5' 7"	scar on wrist & right eye	BoD		
7	553	Sorrell	Fritz	27	bright	5' 6"	scar on neck	BoD		
7	554	Green	Emily	27	bright	5' 2"	no scar	BoD		
7	555	Green	M E	8	bright	4' 3"	no scar	BoD		
7	556	Carpenter	Elizabeth	26	bright	5' 5½"	no scar	BoD		
7	557	Sorrell	Jas	20	bright	5' 5"	no scar	BoD	14 Sept 1850	E&ftbc[398]

P #	Reg. #	Name, Last	Name, First	Age	Color	Ht.	Marks or scars	BF or Eman	Date of Register	When Cert.
							"Northumberland County, Virginia Register of Free Negroes 1849-1858."			
7	558	Martin	Eliza	26	bright	6'	no scar	BoD		
7	559	Sorrell	Wynder	38	bright	6'	scar over left eye	BoD		
8	560	Sorrell	William	15	bright	4' 9"	no scar			
8	561	Thomas	Spencer	53	black	6' 6"	having six fingers on each hand	BF[N]		
8	562	Wood	Maz	24	dark	4' 1"	crooked fingers on left hand	BF[N]	[16 Oct 1850]	Ebtc[399]
8	563	Jones	Winny	45	black	5'	scar on right arm	BF[N]		Do
8	564	Wood	Susan	9	light	4' 2"	nvmos	BF[N]		Do
8	565	Wood	Margaret	6	light	3' 3"	nsom	BF[N]		Do
9	566	Hurst[240]	John	40		5' 5¼"	scar on the right cheek[400]	BF[N]	Renew #240[104]	
9	567	Kelly	Nancy	25	bright	5' 2" & ¾	mark or scar right side[401]	BF[N]		Ebtc&fc[402]
9	568	Kelly	Susan	24	~~dark light~~ light	~~5' 3¼"~~ 5' 3¼"	nmos	BF[N]		Do
9	569	Kelly	Martha	20	light	5' ¾"	burn on left eye	BF[N]		Do
9	570	Kelly	De Ella	18	light	5' 5¼"	scar on under part [403]	BF[N]		Do
9	571	Kelly	Peter	17	light	5' 6½"	nmos	BF[N]		Do

[104]Renewed from Register No. 240.

68

P #	Reg. #	Name, Last	Name, First	Age	Color	Ht.	Marks or scars	BF or Eman	Date of Register	When Cert.
							"Northumberland County, Virginia Register of Free Negroes 1849-1858."			
9	572	Kelly	John Nathaniel	15	Dark	5' 6"	nmos	BF[N]		Do
9	573	Nickins	Judith	30	bright	5' 4 ¾"	fore great tooth cut	BF[L]		
9	574	Nickins	Barton Andrew	11	bright	4' 3"	nmos	BF[L]		
9	575	Nickins	Sophronia Ellen	8	bright	3' 11 ¾"	nmos	BF[L]		
9	576	Nickins	Lombard Lucious	6	bright	3' 6" & ¾	nmos	BF[N]		
10	577	Nickens	Bartholomew Carter	3	light	3' 1"	nmos	BF[N]		
10	578	Nickens	Robert Overton	9 m	bright	IITA	nmos	BF[N]		
10	579	Ritch	Judith	40	Dark	5' 1 ¾"	small scar middle [404]	BF[405]		
10	580	Veny	Nancy	40	light	5' 6¼"	nmos	BF[L]		
10	581	Kelly	Sally	23	bright	5' 1¼"	mark on right[406]	BF[L]		
10	582	Veny	Mordacia	8	dark	3' 11"	nmos	BF[L]		
10	583	Veny	Ashwill	6	dark	3' 4½"	nmos	BF[L]		
10	584	Veny	Maranda Ann	4	dark	3'	nmos	BF[L]		
10	585	Veny	Catharine	12	light	5'	nmos	BF[L]		
11	586	Veny	Simon	11	light	4' 6"	scar in forehead[407]	BF[L]		
11	587	Veney	Nancy	6	dark	3' 11"	nsom	BF[L]		

	"Northumberland County, Virginia Register of Free Negroes 1849-1858."									
P #	Reg. #	Name, Last	Name, First	Age	Color	Ht.	Marks or scars	BF or Eman	Date of Register	When Cert.
13	606	Sorrell	James	3 yr	bright	IITA	Burn on inside[412]	BF[N]		
13	607	Garnton	Nancy	23	bright	5' 2"	2 scars on right cheek	BF[N]		
13	608	Garnton	William James	5	light	3' 2"	nmos	BF[N]		
13	609	Thomas	Ann	28	bright	5' 3"	Scar in right thumb			
13	610	Sank	Nancy	28	dark	5'	Scar in left rist			
13	611	Green	John Westly	11	light	4' 6"	no scar etc.			Ebtc&fc[413]
13	612	Green	Henry	7	light	3' 11"	no scar etc			Do
13	613	Sank	John	14	dark	4' 8¼"	no mark etc.			
13	614	Sank	Henry	9	dark	3' 11½"	scar across his neck			
13	615	Sank	William	14	light	4' 11"	small scar on left rist			
13	616	Sank	Angaline	15	bright	5' 11"	scar over right eye			
14	617	Sank	Thomas	50	light	5' 8"	3[d] finger in right hand bent			
14	618	Sank	Louisianna	7	dark	3' 5"	no scar			
14	619	Sank	Matilda	30	light	5' ½"	no mark			
14	620	Sorrell	Sarah Elizabeth	7	dark	3' 10½"				
14	621	Sorrell	Thomas Richard	5	dark	3' 4½"	no mark			
14	622	Sorrell	Virginia	3	light	2' 11½"	no mark			

P #	Reg. #	Name, Last	Name, First	Age	Color	Ht.	Marks or scars	BF or Eman	Date of Register	When Cert.
							"Northumberland County, Virginia Register of Free Negroes 1849-1858."			
14	623	Sorrell	Olivia	9 m	light	IITA	no mark			
14	624	Weaver	Elizabeth	14	bright	5'	no mark		[15 Oct 1850]	Ebtc [414]
14	625	Thomas	Doris	19	dark	5' 7½"	no mark			
14	626	Weaver	Margaret	11	bright	4' 5½"	scar on right side forehead			Do
14	627	Weaver	Joseph	8	bright	4' 3¼"	no mark			Do
15	628	Weaver	Judith	7	bright	3' 7"	no mark		[14 Oct 1850]	Ebc&fc [415]
15	629	Weaver	Emily	4	bright	2" 8"	no mark			Do
15	630	Thomas	Henry	13	dark	5'	no mark		[14 Oct 1850]	Ebtc&fc [416]
15	631	Thomas	Oscar	11	dark	4' 8"	no mark			Do
15	632	Thomas	Rufus	8	light	4' 5"	sixth finger from each hand cut			Do
15	633	Thomas	Nancy	40	light	5' 1"	no mark			Do
15	634	Thomas	Ferdinand	9	dark	4' 4½"	6 fingers in left hand			Do
15	635	Martin	Mahala	47	light	5' 2¾"	no mark	BF[N]	14th Oct. 1850	E&fc [417]
15	636	Keiser	Ferdinand	10	bright	3' 10½"	no mark	BF[N]	14th Oct. 1850	E&fc [418]
15	637	Keiser	Francis	18	bright	5' 3½"	scar in right cheek	BF	14th Oct. 1850	E&fc [419]

P #	Reg. #	Name, Last	Name, First	Age	Color	Ht.	Marks or scars	BF or Eman	Date of Register	When Cert.
							"Northumberland County, Virginia Register of Free Negroes 1849-1858."			
16	638	Sank	Eliza	30	dark	5' ¾"	moal on back of the neck	BF[N]	14th Oct. 1850.	Ebtc&fc [420]
16	639	Sank	Maranda	14	bright	5' 2 ¾"	moal on right cheek	BF[N]	14th Oct. 1850.	Ebtc&fc [421]
16	640	Sank	Isabella	21	dark	5' ½"	scar across nose and[422]	BF[N]	14th Oct. 1850.	Ebtc&fc[423]
16	641	Sank	Betty	31	dark	5'	scar on left rist and [424]	BF[N]	14th Oct. 1850.	Ebtc&fc[425]
16	642	Sorrell	Judith	45	bright	5' 2"	no mark			
16	643	Sorrell	Ethelbert	9	bright	4' 4"	scar on right ear			
16	644	Sorrell	James	60	light	5' 6½"	no mark			
16	645	Sorrell	Henry	7	bright	4'	no mark			
16	646	Credit ~~Sorrell~~	William	15	bright	5' ½"	no mark			
16	647	Sorrell	Cyrus	16	bright	5'½"	no mark			
16	648	Sorrell	Placidia	15	light	5'	cut on neck	BF	14th Oct 1850.	Ebtc&fc [426]
17	649	Carpenter	Mary Jane	9	bright	4'4"	no mark	BF	14th Oct 1850	E&fc [427]
17	650	Carpenter	Elizabeth Francis	7	bright	4'	no mark	D°	D°	D°
17	651	Carpenter	Rufus Henry	5	bright	3'4½"	no mark	D°	D°	D°
17	652	Roberson	George Oscar	7	dark	3'7"	no mark			

P #	Reg. #	Name, Last	Name, First	Age	Color	Ht.	Marks or scars	BF or Eman	Date of Register	When Cert.
							"Northumberland County, Virginia Register of Free Negroes 1849-1858."			
17	653	Roberson	Lucy Ann	4	dark	3' 5"	a six[th] finger ? from left hand			
17	654	Roberson	Olivia Jean	3	light dark	3'5"	no mark			
17	655	Roberson	Emily Ann	9 m	dark	IITA	no mark			
17	656	Nickins	Jane	35	light	5' 3"	burns on right hand & thumb			
17	657	Nickins	Francis	19	light	5' 6½"	no mark			
17	658	Nickins	Dolly Ann	15	light	5' 1½"	no mark			
17	659	Nickins	Mary	11	dark	4' 4"	scar in forehead			
18	660	Casity	Samuel	57	black	5' ½"	scar in roots of the hair[428]		[14 Oct 1850]	Ebtc&fc[429]
18	661	Casity	Igatus	26	dark	5' 2"	small scar in back of right hand			Do
18	662	Casity	Samuel Jr.	15	black	5' 1"	scar over right eye			Do
18	663	Casity	James	18	black	4' 1"	no mark			Do
18	664	Casity	John	10	black	4'	no mark			Do
18	665	Casity	Lidia Ann	14	black	4' 10"	no mark			Do
18	666	Casity	Emeline	13	black	4' 11"	scar in roots of hair[430]			Do
18	667	Casity	William Henry	10	bright	3' 11"	no mark			Do
18	668	Casity	Judith Ann	6	black	3' 3½"	no mark			Do

P #	Reg. #	Name, Last	Name, First	Age	Color	Ht.	Marks or scars	BF or Eman	Date of Register	When Cert.
							"Northumberland County, Virginia Register of Free Negroes 1849-1858."			
18	669	Casity	Sarah Elizabeth	3	bright	2' 11"	no mark			Do
19	670	Casity	Elizabeth	2	dark	IITA	no mark		[14 Oct 1850]	Ebtc&fc[431]
19	671	Casity	William Rily	10	dark	4'	no mark			Do
19	672	Casity	Mary	40	black	5' 2"	scar in right rist			Do
19	673	Spriddle	Lucy	30	light	5' 5"	no mark			Do
19	674	Weaver	Elizabeth	27	bright	5' 5¼"	no mark		[14 Oct 1850]	Ebtc&fc[432]
19	675	Weaver	Loringer Dikes	5	light	3' 6¼"	no mark			Do
19	676	Weaver	Mary Francis	3	bright	3' 3"	no mark			Do
19	677	Weaver	Whittendon	12	dark	4' 8"	no mark			
19	678	Hubbard	Mary	25	dark	5' 1"	scar in forehead & left hand		[14 Oct 1850]	Ebtc&fc[433]
20		[missing number]								
20	680	Hubbard	Agnes	13	dark	4' 6"	scar in left side of forehead		[14 Oct 1850]	Ebtc&fc[434]
20	681	Hubbard	Robert	12	dark	4' 1½"	scar in left side of forehead			Do
20	682	Hubbard	John Nathaniel	10	dark	4'	no mark			Do

"Northumberland County, Virginia Register of Free Negroes 1849-1858."									
P #	Reg. #	Name, Last	Name, First	Age	Color	Ht.	Marks or scars	BF or Eman	Date of Register	When Cert.
20	683	Cole?	Sally	18	bright	5' 2¾"	no mark			
20	684	Jackson	Morris	40	dark	5' 8"	scar on right hand			
20	685	Jackson	Mary	37	light	5' 5¼"	scar on right cheek			
20	686	Jackson	Margaret	9	dark	4'	pitted with small pox			
20	687	Owens	Elizabeth	10	bright	3' 11½"	no mark			
20	688	Armstead	Frances	19	light	5' 3"	scar on back of left hand			
20	689	Blundon	John	15	dark	5' 1"	no mark		[14 Oct 1850]	Ebtc&fc[435]
21	690	Blundon	Samuel	16	light	4' 4"	no mark		[14 Oct 1850]	Ebtc&fc[436]
21	691	Blundon	Virginia	14	bright	4' 8"	no mark			
21	692	Blundon	Sarah Ann	15	bright	5' ½"	no mark			
21	693	Thomas	Jane	26	black	5' 2¾"	left eye out & scar [437]			
21	694	Thomas	Benjamin	47	black	5' 11"	scar in forehead			
21	695	Carpenter	Alexander	21	bright	6"	much freckled			
21	696	Day	William	52	light	5' 6½"	no mark			
21	697	Ewell	Elizabeth	15	light	5' 2¾	mark on right arm		[14 Oct 1850]	Ebtc&fc[438]
21	698	Ewell	Mary Ann	14	bright	5'	mark in right cheek			Do
21	699	Ewell	Warner	37	light	5' 8"	scar in right leg			Do

75

P #	Reg. #	Name, Last	Name, First	Age	Color	Ht.	Marks or scars	BF or Eman	Date of Register	When Cert.
							"Northumberland County, Virginia Register of Free Negroes 1849-1858."			
22	700	Ewell	Elizabeth & child Jane	38	bright	5' 2½"	scar in right rist		[15 Oct 1850]	Ebtc&fc[439]
22	701	Ewell	Eliza June	15	bright	5'	no mark			Do
22	702	Ewell	Lavalia Ann	14	light	5' 5"	no mark			
22	703	Ewell	Frances	12	light	4' 4"	scar in top of head			Do
22	704	Ewell	Roxy	9	light	4' 2"	scar in left cheek			
22	705	Ewell	Matthais	7	light	3' 6"	no mark			
22	706	Ewell	William Henry	2	light	3'	no mark			Do
22	707	Stanford	Sally	40	light	5'	scar on left cheek	BF[N]		Ebtc&fc[440]
22	708	Weaver	Nancy	50	light	5' 4"	scar in left eye & left wrist	Do		
22	709	Weaver	Elijah	52	dark	5' 4"	no mark	Do		
23	710	Ewell	Piney	38	light	5' 3"	scar on left wrist	BF[N]	[11 Nov 1850]	Ebtc&fc[441]
23	711	Ewell	Tho[s]	16	light	4' 10"	no marks	Do		Do
23	712	Ewell	Eliza Ann	9	light	4'	scar over right eye	Do		Do
23	713	Ewell	John H.	8	light	3' 10"	nsom	Do		Do
23	714	Ewell	Judith M.	3	light	2' 10"	no mark	Do		
23	715	Blundon	Alice	35	dark	5' 2"	scar on left arm	Do		
23	716	Blundon	Rufus	11	bright	4' 8"	no scar	Do		

76

P #	Reg. #	Name, Last	Name, First	Age	Color	Ht.	Marks or scars	BF or Eman	Date of Register	When Cert.
							"Northumberland County, Virginia Register of Free Negroes 1849-1858."			
23	717	Jackson	Harriet	30	bright	5' 3"	a small scar on forehead	Do		
23	718[105]	Moore	Daniel	36	bright	3' 8"	no mark or scar	Do		
24	719	Ashton	Joshua	16	light	5' 2"	nvmos	BF[N]		
24	720	Sorrell[87]	Edward	57	bright	5'10"	mark on skin & anke	Do	[28th Nov 1850]	28th Nov[442]
24	721	Casity ?	Lucinda	21	light	5' 4"	nvmos	Do		
24	722	Laws	Beverly	24	light	5' 10"	nvmos	Do	[11 Feb. 1851]	11 Feb[443]
24	723[106]	Laws[451]	Robert	30	bright	5' 8"	nvmos	Do	[23rd April 1851]	23rd April[444]
24	#724	Carpenter	Betsy	32	bright	5' 2"?	small mark left hand[445]	Do	[10 June 1851]	10 June[446]
24	725	Wood	Albert	23	bright	5' 8" ¾	nvmos	Do		
24	726	Laws	Baldin	31	light	5' 9" ¾	nvmos	Do		Ebtc&fc[447]
24	727	Toulson	Eliza Ann	20	dark	5' 2"	nvmos	Do		Ebtc&fc[448]
24	728	Day	James	14	light	5' 5½"	nvmos	Do		
25	729	Toulson	Maritchia Ann	38	dark	5' 2"	has scar on forehead	BF[N]		

[105]formerly 447.

[106]No. 723 formerly 451.

P #	Reg. #	Name, Last	Name, First	Age	Color	Ht.	Marks or scars	BF or Eman	Date of Register	When Cert.
							"Northumberland County, Virginia Register of Free Negroes 1849-1858."			
25	730	Laws	Lindsey	20	bright	5' 8"	nvmos	BF[N]	[8 Sept 1851]	Ebtc&fc[449]
25	731	Laws	Daniel	53	light	5' 7"	nvmos	BF[NL]		
25	732	Cornish	William	23	light	5' 8⅓"	nvmos	BF[N]	[8 Sept 1851]	Ebtc&fc[450]
25	733	Bee	Eliza	26	bright	5' 2"	nvmos	BF[N]	[8 Sept 1851]	Ebtc&fc[451]
25	734	Laws	Nancy	22	bright	5' 4"	nvmos	BF[N]	[8 Sept 1851]	Ebtc&fc[452]
25	735	Laws	Margaret	16	bright	5' 4"	nvmos	BF[N]		
25	736	Laws	Martha	14	bright	5' 0"	nvmos	BF[N]	[8 Sept 1851]	Ebtc&fc[453]
26	737	Laws	Mary	11	bright	4' 7"	nvmos	BF[N]	[8 Sept 1851]	Ebtc&fc[454]
26	738	Bee	Aleyndia	5	bright	3' 5"	nvmos	BF[N]	[8 Sept 1851]	Ebtc&fc[455]
26	739	Bee	Olivia	4	bright	3' 1'	nvmos	BF[N]	[8 Sept 1851]	Ebtc&fc[456]
26	740	Bee	Calvin	4	dark	3' 1"	nvmos	BF[N]	[8 Sept 1851]	Ebtc&fc[457]
26	741	Bee	Narcissas	2	bright	2' 9"	nvmos	BF[N]	[8 Sept 1851]	Ebtc&fc[458]
26	742	Laws	Peggy	50	bright	5' 5"	nvmos	Do	[8 Sept 1851]	Ebtc&fc[459]

P #	Reg. #	Name, Last	Name, First	Age	Color	Ht.	Marks or scars	BF or Eman Register	Date of Register	When Cert.
26	743	Drake	Judy (Roxy)	32	bright	5' 4"	nvmos	BFN	[13 Oct 1851]	Ebtc&fc[460]
26	744	Bee	James	26	bright	5' 3½"	nvmos	BFN	[13 Oct 1851]	Ebtc&fc[461]
27	745	Drake	William Richard	9	bright	4' 5"	Lame in right leg	BFN	[13 Oct 1851]	Ebtc&fc[462]
27	746	Drake	Henry	7	dark	3' 11½"	nvmos	BFN	[13 Oct 1851]	Ebtc&fc[463]
27	747	Drake	Addison	5	bright	5' 1"	nvmos	BFN	[13 Oct 1851]	Ebtc&fc[464]
27	748	Drake	Susan	1	light	2' 7½"	nvmos	BFN	[13 Oct 1851]	Ebtc&fc[465]
27	749	Bee	Hiram	55	bright	5' 1"	nvmos	BFN	[13 Oct 1851]	Ebtc&fc[466]
27	750	Cattrill	Ann	4 m	bright	2' h	nvmos	BFN	[13 Oct 1851]	Ebtc&fc[467]
27	751	Bee	Anna Eliza	22	bright	5' 6½" h	nvmos	BFN	[13 Oct 1851]	Ebtc&fc[468]
27	752	Bee	Sady (Polly)	22	bright	5' 6½" h	nvmos	BFN	[10 Nov 1851]	Ebtc&fc[469]
28	753	Bell	William	14	dark	4' 10"	nvmos	BFN	[10 Nov 1851]	10 Nov[470]
28	754	Drake	Addison	34	bright	5' 10"	scar on left arm	BF[471]	[Dec. 8, 1851]	Dec. 8, [472]

"Northumberland County, Virginia Register of Free Negroes 1849-1858."

"Northumberland County, Virginia Register of Free Negroes 1849-1858."									
P #	Reg. #	Name, Last	Name, First	Age	Color	Ht.	Marks or scars	BF or Eman	Date of Register	When Cert.
28	755	Bee	Elizabeth	21	bright	5' 2"	nvmos	BF[N]		
28	756	Betts	Thomas D.	13	bright	4' 8"	scar on left side of neck[473]	BF[N]	[July 12th 1852]	July 12th [474]
28	757	Toulson	John	19	dark	5' 5"	nvmos	BF[N]		
28	758	Reid	Maria	42	dark	5' 6½"	a small scar on each hand	BF[N]		
28	759	Toulson	Thomas	22	bright	5' 11"	nvmos	BF[N]		
28	760	Bee	Margaret	20	tawny	5' 6"	scar on left hand	BF[N]		
28	761	Henderson	John	22	tawny	5' 4"	nvmos	BF[N]		
28	~~762~~	~~King~~	~~Thornton~~	~~22~~	~~light~~	~~5' 8"~~	nvmos			
29[107]	762	~~Jones=~~	~~Amstead~~	~~27~~	~~bright~~	~~5' 8"~~	~~scar on the right cheek~~	~~BF[N]~~		
29	762			30	bright	5' 10 ¾"	small scar on right cheek[475]	BF[N]		Pap. del.[476]
29	763	Jackson	Philip	27	dark	5' 10"	nvmos	BF[N]		Pap. del.[477]
29	764	Nickens	Armstead	20	dark	5' 10"	scar in left rist	BF[N]		Pap. del. to
29	765	Pointer	R.	20	dark	5' 9"	nvmos	BF[N]		
29	766	Reid	W[m]	21	dark	5' 5"	nvm	BF[N]		
29	767	Toulson	W[m]	20	Bright	5' 10"	scar on right arm	BF[N]		
29	768	Toulson	Armen	21	Bright	4'	scar on forehead	BF[N]		

[107]On this entire page, the color column comes before the age column. Also, #762 is repeated from page #28.

"Northumberland County, Virginia Register of Free Negroes 1849-1858."									
P #	Reg. #	Name, Last	Name, First	Age	Color	Ht.	Marks or scars	BF or Eman	Date of Register	When Cert.
29	769	Haw	James	24	dark	5' 7"	nvm	BF^N		
29	770	Bee	Oswald	27	dark	5' 8	nvm	BF^N		
30[108]	771	King	David	21	yellow	5' 5"	scar on the left thumb	BF^N		
30	772	Day	Elie	20	dark	5' 8" h	nvs	BF^N		
30	773	Kelly	Joseph	21	dark	5' 11½"h	nvs	BF^N		
30	774	Fleet	Sally	22	yellow	5' 1" h	scar on the right ear	BF^N		Ebtc&fc[478]

---

[108]On this entire page, the color column comes before the age column.

<td colspan="10" align="center">"Northumberland County, Virginia Register of Free Negroes 1849-1858."</td>
P #	Reg. #	Name, Last	Name, First	Age	Color	Ht.	Marks or scars	BF or Eman	Date of Register	When Cert.
29	765	Pointer	R.	20	dark	5' 9"	nvmos	BF^N		
29	766	Reid	W^m	21	dark	5' 5"	nvm	BF^N		
29	767	Toulson	W^m	20	Bright	5' 10"	scar on right arm	BF^N		
29	768	Toulson	Armen	21	Bright	4'	scar on forehead	BF^N		
29	769	Haw	James	24	dark	5' 7"	nvm	BF^N		
29	770	Bee	Oswald	27	dark	5' 8	nvm	BF^N		
30[108]	771	King	David	21	yellow	5' 5"	scar on the left thumb	BF^N		
30	772	Day	Elie	20	dark	5' 8" h	nvs	BF^N		
30	773	Kelly	Joseph	21	dark	5' 11½"h	nvs	BF^N		
30	774	Fleet	Sally	22	yellow	5' 1" h	scar on the right ear	BF^N		Ebtc&fc[478]

---

[108]On this entire page, the color column comes before the age column.

1. a scar on the breast occasioned by the bite of a horse.

2. Examined & found correct 13th Jany 1806 & decd Co[l] Ball ?.

3. a scar on the left hand above the little finger.

4. Examined & found correct 12 Mar 1806 cert. & del..

5. Emancipated by John Blundon's Will recorded in North[d] District Court.

6. Examined & found correct 9th June 1806.

7. Examined & found correct 9th June 1806.

8. scar on the left arm about 6 inches above the wrist..

9. a scar on the right arm about four inches from the wrist.

10. Examined & found correct ? 12 Mar. 1806 cert. & deliv[d.]

11. scar on the right ?[m] occasioned ?[m] burn.

12. Emancipated by the will of John Bar.

13. Examined & found correct 10th March 1807.

14. very much pitted with the small pox, a scar under each ear & one under the chinn occasioned thereby.

15. Born Free of a White Mother.

16. Examined & found correct 14th Sept. 1807.

17. Emancipated by the will of John Blundon recorded in North[d] District Court.

18. native of Pennsylvania & an indented servant of Col[o] James Moore late of Philadelphia.

84

19. Black & of a yellowish cast.

20. exam^d & found correct 9 May 1809 cert^d & cert deld.

21. Examd & found correct June 1809 -- copd & deld 4th Sept 1809.

22. 10 October 1809.

23. Ex^d & found correct 13th Nov. 1809.

24. examd & found correct July 9 1810 -- cert^d deld.

25. Examined & found correct 8 Oct° 1810. cert deld 15 Oct° 1810 attested by John Cralle ?

26. ex^d and found correct deld 14 Aug^t.

27. Born in the state of Pennsylvania & emancipated by the laws of the state for the abolition of slavery & bro't to this state by Col° James Moore.

28. Only a portion of the page showing the numbers of the free blacks remains. [Note written by W. Preston Haynie, attached to photocopy.]

29. a scar on the right side of the forehead & a small scar in the right arm above the elbow.

30. a small not on the left side of his forehead -- a scar on the right knee occasioned by a burn -- the left ankle somewhat twisted.

31. Liberated by deed of emancipation, by Cyrus Sutton of North^d County.

32. Examined & found correct 13 Jany 1812 cop^d & del^d 13 Jany.

33. Examined & found correct 13 Jany 1812 cop^d & del^d 13 Jany.

34. cert^d & deld^d 13th July 1812 -- attested by R. Edwards.

35. a scar between the thumb & forefinger of the right hand.

36. cert^d & deld^d 13th July 1812 attested by R. Edwards.

37. marked on the left wrist with India ink w.c. -- c.

38. cert^d 12 Oct^o 1812 -- cert -- attested by J. Cockarell.

39. Emancipated by the will of John Blundon recorded in the District Court of North^d.

40. cert^d to be correct 11 Jany 1813.

41. small scar over the right temple from a burn.

42. Liberated by the will of John Turner.

43. a small scar under his right eye near his nose somewhat bowlegged.

44. Liberated by the will of Mary Elliston.

45. cert^d & delivered 16 June 1813 attested by.

46. a scar on the inside of her right? breast.

47. cert^d to be correct 11 Jany 1813.

48. His left hand much injured by a burn.

49. a scar on the right side of his head.

50. cer^d to be correct July 1813 cert. attested by W. Ball.

51. [number supplied], page torn and number missing.

52. a black mark or mole on the left arm.

53. Exam^d & cert^d 14 June 1814.

54. [ns], page torn and number missing.

55. a small black spot over the right eye.

56. a scar on the fleshy part of the right leg.

57. a scar on the right side of the neck.

58. Born in Pennsylvania and emancipated by the laws of the state for the abolition of slavery -- was bro^t to this state by Col. James Moore.

59. a small scar on the underside of the right arm.

60. a small scar on the inn side of her right arm.

61. a small scar on the back of the left hand.

62. a burn on the back of the right hand.

63. a small scar on the back of the left hand by a burn.

64. Born a slave in North^d County -- & liberated by the will of Caleb Redman.

65. 9 Oct^o 1815 Exam^d & found correct -- copy attested by Jo. Ball ?

66. Ex^d & found correct 11 May 1815.

67. Ex^d & found correct 11 May 1815.

68. Born of a white woman in North^d County.

69. 90 formerly 47.

70. Number supplied ?^{M}.

71. Number supplied ?^{M}.

72. Register exam^d & found correct 12 Jany 1818.

73. 11 Sept. 1815 -- cop^d attested.

74. 92 formerly 3.

75. a considerable space between her upper fore teeth.

76. a small scar on the underside of the right arm.

77. Register exam^d 8 July 1816 & f^d correct Attested by M. Lamkin.

78. Register examined & found correct 9th July 1816 attested by J L Chinn.

79. ex^d by the C^L 8 July 1810 & f^d correct.

80. Register examined & found correct 8 July 1816 -- copy attested by J. H. Fallin.

81. Emancipated by Col^o Wm. Ball. by deed.

82. Register exam^d & found correct 14 July 1817.

83. a mark from the cut of an ax on the left shoulder.

84. Emancipated by Cyrus Sutton.

85. Register ex^d & found correct 12 Jany 1818.

86. a scar near the upper joint of the middle finger of the left hand.

87. Register exam^d & f^d correct 14 July 1817.

88. 106 formerly 93.

89. Register exam^d & f^d correct 14 July 1817.

90. Register exam^d & f^d correct 14 July 1817.

91. a considerable space between her upper foreteeth.

92. Register exam^d & f^d correct 14 July 1817.

93. Register exam^d & f^d correct 14 July 1817.

94. a scar on the right side of the neck.

95. Born in Pennsylvania emancipated by the laws of the for the abolition of slavery was brot to this state Col James Moore.

96. a small scar on the right wrist from a cut.

97. Register ex^d 8 June 1818 & found correct.

98. a small scar running into the left eyebrow.

99. Examined & found correct 8 June 1818 cert & attested by W. Gordon & deld^d 10 June 1818.

100. Emancipated by Col^o W. Ball by deed.

101. Register exam^d & found correct 11 Augt cert. attested by W. Jett & deld^d 21 Sept 1818.

102. a small black spot near the right eye.

103. Emancipated by Col. W. Ball by deed.

104. a small round wattle near his right ear.

105. emancipated by deed by Robert Carter late of West^d County.

106. a flesh mould on the back of the neck.

107. Name does not appear in this form on the original.

108. Name does not appear in this form on the original.

109. Name does not appear in this form on the original.

110. Name does not appear in this form on the original.

111. Born of Free Parents in Norfolk.

112. examined & found correct 9th August 1819. Attested by M. Lamkin cert^d and del.

113. The right eye out no other particular marks.

114. 125 formerly 115.

115. Register exam^d & f^d correct 13 June 1820.

116. the forefinger of the right hand much scared.

117. a scar across the right side of her lower lip.

118. a scar near his right eye adjoining the nose.

119. Examined & found correct 16 May cert^d attested by Jas Basye.

120. a burn on the left hand between the thumb & forefinger.

121. Liberated by the will of John R. Harrison.

122. Examd & found correct ? 14 May cert^d.

123. 150 formerly 116.

124. Liberated by the late Col^o Wm Ball.

125. Exm^d 13 May 1823 & found correct attested by Wm Henderson.

126. Exam^d ? 9th June 1823 & found correct attested by Joseph Basye & del^d 10 June 1823.

127. Ex^d 9th June 1823 & found correct attested by Jos. Basye & del^d 10 June.

128. Ex^d 9 June 1823 & found correct attested by Joseph Basye & del^d 10 June.

129. a scar on his nose between his eyes and 1 over the left eye.

130. Ex^d 16 July 1823 & found correct. Attested by James Smith Gent -- & del^d 15th.

131. Born of Free Parents in West^d County.

132. Born of free parents in Essex County.

133. Liberated by the late Col^o Wm Ball.

134. Exam^d 12 Jany & cert^d -- attested by Doctr. ? Basye.

135. Exam^d by Court 9 Feby 1824 & cert^d -- attested by Wm Jett Gent.

136. born of free parents in North^d C^o & was bound by O. of poor to G. G.[Y] Beane.

137. Exam^d by court 8th March 1824 -- & cert^d attested by Doc'r Ja^s Basye Gent.

138. a small black spot near the right eye.

139. the letters HN on the left arm & an anchor on the hand.

140. Ex^d 10 May & cert^d -- attested by Doct. Basye Gent.

141. Ex^d 10 May & cer^d -- attested by Wm Harding Gent.

142. Ex^d by the court & cert^d to be correct 11 Oct 1824 -- cert attested by.

143. Judy Day is presented her children James Polly Sally & Betty between the ages of 13 & 6.

144. Judy Day is presented her children James Polly Sally & Betty between the ages of 13 & 6.

145. Judy Day is presented her children James Polly Sally & Betty between the ages of 13 & 6.

146. born of free parents in North^d county & served apprenticeship with G Y Beane.

147. Exam^d by Court and found correct 15th March 1825 & attested by Jo. Deshields Gent.

148. Exam^d & found correct 10 May 1825 -- Cert. attested by Jo. Deshields.

149. the forefinger of the right hand much scarred.

150. Ex^d by C^t 10 May 1825 -- Cert. attested by Jo. Basye -- Gt.

151. several scars on the left side his face.

152. Examined by court 12 Sept. 1825 -- cert attested by Jo^s Basye Gent^l --

153. Exam^d by ct. 12 Sept 1825. Cert^d attested by Jo Deshields Gt.

154. Ex^d by ct 13 Feb 1826 & found correct -- cert attested by Jo Deshields Gent.

155. Exam^d & found correct 12 March 1826 & cert^d 13 March 1826 & cert^d attested by Jas Basye Gent.

156. Exam^d by court & found correct 9 May 1826 & cert attested by _____ Gent.

157. Born of free parents in Essex County Va.

158. Exam^d by court & found correct 9 May 1826 & cert attested by Wm Harding ? Gent.

159. Emancipated by deed by Robt. Carter late of West^d County.

160. Exam^d & found correct 9 Oct^o 1826 & cert^d attested by Wm Harding Gent.

161. Born of free parents in Richmond County.

162. Emancipated by Cyrus Sutton, dec^d.

163. Examined by court & found correct 9 Oct° 1826 Attested by Tho Hughlett Gent.

164. Exam^d & found correct attested by Wm Harding Gent 9 Oct° 1826.

165. Emancipated by Cyrus Sutton dec^d.

166. Exam^d 14 Nov 1826 -- cert attested by Jo. Deshields Gent.

167. Ex^d and found correct 13 Aug 1827 cert signed by J Deshields Gent.

168. Exam^d 12 Feb 1827 & cert to be correct attested by J Basye Gent.

169. Examined & cert^d 9 April 1827 attested by Jo Basye -- Gent.

170. Ex^d & found correct 9 July 1827 -- cert. attested by Jo Deshields Gent.

171. Exam^d & certified 11 June 1827 -- cert attested by Jno Middleton Gent.

172. Ex^d 11 June 1827 & cert^d -- cert attested by Jn° Middleton Esq.

173. scar on the breast & 3 fingers of right injured.

174. Exam^d & cert^d by Court 10th Sept 1827 -- attested by Wm Harding Gt.

175. Ex^d & found correct 11 March 1828 copy attested by Jo^s Deshields Gl.

176. Ex^d & found correct 9 June 1828 copy attested by Jo^s Deshields Gl.

177. Ex^d & found correct 9 June 1828 copy attested by Jo^s Deshields Gl.

178. Ex^d 8th June 1829 & found correct by the court attested by Jo^s Deshields Gl.

179. Examined by the court 12th November 1828.

180. a lump on the breast occasioned by a cut.

181. born of free parents in Richmond Coty.

182. Ex^d 12 May 1829 & found correct copy attested by Jas Deshields Gent.

183. Examined by the court 10 August 1829 and found correct attested by <u>Joseph Basye</u> Gent.

184. a flesh mark below the breast bone & another on the left arm.

185. a scar between the eyes & on the right eyebrow & left cheek.

186. Exam^d 11 May 1829. & found correct.

187. a scar in the forehead & a flesh mark on the right arm.

188. Examined 12 May 1829 & found correct copy attested by Jos. Basye Gent.

189. Exam^d 13 May 1829 & found correct.

190. liberated by Tho Hurst.

191. Exam^d 8th June 1829 & found correct by the court -- attested by M. Lamkin Gent.

192. Exam^d 8th June 1829 by the court & found correct attested by M. Lamkin Gent.

193. Examined by the court 8 June 1829 & found correct attested by Wm Jett Gent.

194. born of free parents in Caroline County.

195. Examd by the court 10 Augt 1829 & found correct attested by Jo. Deshields Gent.

196. Examined by the court 10 Augt 1829 and found correct attested by Jos Deshields Gent.

197. Examined by the court 10 Augt 1829 and found correct.

198. Examined by the court 10 Augt 1829 and found correct.

199. Examined by the court 10 Augt 1829 and found correct.

200. Examined by the court 10 Augt 1829 and found correct.

201. Examined by the court 10 Augt 1829 and found correct. Attested by Wm. Harding Jr. Gent.

202. Examined by the court 8 March 1830 & found correct. Attested by J. Blackwell Gent.

203. Examined by the court 12 Oct^o 1829. and found correct. Attested by Jos. Deshields Gent.

204. Examined by the court 12 Oct^o 1829. and found correct. Attested by Jos. Deshields Gent.

205. Examined by the court 9th November 1829. Attested by Wm Harding jp Gent.

206. Examined by the court 8 March 1830 & found correct. Attested by

207. Examined by the court 8 March 1830 & found correct. Attested by Wm Harding Jr. Gent.

208. Examined by court 14 June 1830 & found correct. Attested by Jos. Basye Gent.

  209. Examined by the court 8 March 1830 & found correct. Attested by J. Blackwell Gent.

210. Examined by the court 8 March 1830 & found correct. Attested by J. Blackwell Gent.

211. Examined by the court 8th March 1830 & found correct.

212. a scar on the right thigh a little above the knee.

213. Examined by the court 8th March 1830 & found correct. Attested by M. Lamkin, Gent.

214. Emancipated by Cyrus Sutton late of North^d.

215. Examined by the court 8th March 1830 & found correct. Attested by John McAdam, Gent.

216. Examined by the court 12 July 1830 & found correct. Attested by Jas. Basye Gent.

217. Examined by the court 15 Mar 1831 & found correct. Attested by Jos. Deshields, Gent.

218. Examined by the court 12 July 1830 & found correct. Attested by M. Lamkin, Gent.

219. Emancipated by Cyrus Sutton.

220. Examined by the court 12 July 1830 & found correct. Attested by Jas. Basye, Gent.

221. Examined by the court 10 Augt 1830 & found correct. Attested by Jas. Deshields, Gent.

222. Examined by the court 15 March 1831 & found correct. Attested by Jas. Deshields, Gent.

223. Examined by the court 8 November 1830 & found correct. Attested by Jas. Deshields, Gent.

224. Examined by the court 8 Nov 1830 & found correct. Attested by Jas. Deshields, Gent.

225. Examined by the court 13 June 1831& found correct. Attested by Jas. Deshields, Gent.

226. Examined by the court 13 Decr 1830 & found correct. Attested by Jas. Basye, Gent.

227. Examined by the court 15 March 1831 & found correct. Attested by Wm Harding, jr. Gent.

228. Examined by the court 15 Mar 1831 & found correct. Attested by Wm Harding, jr. Gent.

229. Examined by the court 15 March 1831 & found correct. Attested by Wm Harding, jr. Gent.

230. Examined by the court 15 March 1831 & found correct. Attested by Wm Harding, jr. Gent.

231. Examined by the court 15 March 1831 & found correct. Attested by Wm Harding, jr. Gent.

232. Ex^d by the court 11 Ap^l 1831 & found correct. Attested by Wm Harding, jr. Gent.

233. Examined by the court 11 Ap^l 1831 & found correct. Attested by Wm Harding, jr. Gent.

234. Examined by the court 11 Ap^l 1831 & found correct. Attested by Wm Harding, jr. Gent.

235. Examined by the court 11 Ap^l 1831 & found correct. Attested by Wm Harding, jr. Gent.

236. Examined by the court 11 Ap^l 1831 & found correct. Attested by Wm Harding, jr. Gent.

237. Examined by the court 11 Ap^l 1831 & found correct. Attested by Wm Harding, jr. Gent.

238. Exd by court 13 June 1831 & found correct. Attested by Jas. Deshields, Gent.

239. Exd by court 13 June 1831 & found correct. Attested by Jas. Deshields, Gent.

240. Exd by court 13 June 1831 & found correct. Attested by Jas. Deshields, Gent.

241. Exd by court 13 June 1831 & found correct. Attested by Jas. Deshields, Gent.

242. Exd by court 13 June 1831 & found correct. Attested by Jas. Deshields, Gent.

243. Exd by court 13 June 1831 & found correct. Attested by Jas. Deshields, Gent.

244. Exd by court 13 June 1831 & found correct. Attested by Jas. Basye Gent.

245. Exd by court 13 June 1831 & found correct. Attested by William Harding Senr. Gent

246. Exd by court 11 July 1831 & found correct. Attested by

247. Exd by court 13th March 1832 & found correct. Attested by J. Deshields, Gent.

248. Examined by court and found correct 15th May 1832. Attested by Wm Harding jr Gent.

249. Exd by court 15 Nov 1831 & found correct. Attested by Jas. Deshields, Gent.

250. Exd by court 15 Nov 1831 & found correct. Attested by Jas. Deshields, Gent.

251. Exd by court 13 Nov 1832 & found correct. Attested by Jas. Deshields, Gent.

252. Examined by the court 13th March [1832] & found to be correct. Attested by Wm. Harding jr Gent.

253. a burn on the right wrist & a scar on the left temple.

254. Examined by the court 13th March [1832] & found to be correct. Attested by J Basye Gent.

255. Examined by the court 13th March 1832 & found to be correct. Attested by J Basye Gent.

256. a dark dimple on chin & a scar in the right knee.

257. Examined by the court 13th March 1832 & found to be correct. Attested by J Basye Gent.

258. Examined by the court 13th March 1832 & found to be correct. Attested by J Basye Gent.

259. 1832 Apl 9. Exd by court & found correct. Attested by Jas. Deshields, Gent.

260. Examined by the court 15th [May 1832] & found to be correct. Attested by Wm Harding jr Gent.

261. Emancipated by the will of Cyrus Sutton.

262. Examined by the court 15th May 1832 & correct. Attested by Wm Harding jr Gent.

263. Exd 9 July 1832 & found correct. Attested by Wm Harding jr Gent.

264. Born of free parents in Gloucester County.

265. 12th March 1833 Exd [&] foun[d] correct. Attested by D. Cox Gent.

266. 12th March 1833 Exd & found correct. Attested by Wm Harding jr Gent.

267. 9 July 1832. Exd & found correct. Attested by T. H. Harvey Gent.

268. 9 July 1832. Exd & found correct.

269. 12th March 1833. Exd & found correct. Attested by D. Cox. Gent.

270. 1833 Dec. 13. Exam^d & found to be correct. Attested by J. Deshields Gent

271. scars on the forehead & on left side of chin bone.

272. 1834 May 12. Ex^d & found correct. Attested by Wm Harding Gent

273. May 12 1834. Ex^d & found to be correct. Attested by Tho. H. Harvey Gent

274. a scar on the forehead & flesh mark on the right arm.

275. 1834 Oct 13. Exam^d & found correct. Attested by J. Deshields Gent

276. 1834 Oct 13. Exam^d & found correct. Attested by J. Deshields Gent

277. 1834 Oct 13. Exam^d & found correct. Attested by J. Deshields Gent

278. 1835 Nov 9. Ex^d & found correct. Attested by J. Deshields Gent

279. Jany 11. 1836. Ex^d & found correct. Attested by Wm Harding Gent

280. Feb 5 1836. Ex^d & found correct. Attested by Tho H Harvey

281. 2 scars on the left side of his face, one on the left hand, and one of the toes of the right foot cutt off.

282. Feb 8 1837. Ex^d & found correct. Attested by Wm Harding Gent

283. 3 scars in the forehead & one on the left side of the cheek.

284. 9 May 1836. Ex^d & found correct. Attested by Wm Harding Gent

285. 13 Mar 1837. Ex^d & found correct. Attested by Wm Harding Gent

286. a flesh mark on the right wrist, a scar caused by a burn on the right side.

287. 12 June 1837. Ex^d & found correct. Attested by Wm Harding . Gent

288. 1838 Mar 12. Exam^d by the court & found correct. Attested by Wm Harding Gent

289. a scar on the left breast occasioned by a burn.

290. August 12th 1839.

291. 1839. Augt 12th. Exam^d by the court & found to be correct. Attested by J. Deshields Gent

292. a scar on the left shoulder & across the left foot.

293. 1839. Augt 12th. Exam^d by the court & found to be correct. Attested by J. Deshields Gent

294. 1839. Augt 12th. Exam^d by the court & found to be correct. Attested by

295. Same in Northd.

296. 1839. Sep 9 -- Examined by the court & found to be correct. Attested by Tho. S. Sydnor, Gent

297. 1839. Sep 9 -- Examined by the court & found to be correct. Attested by Tho. S. Sydnor, Gent

298. 1839. Sep 9 -- Examined by the court & found to be correct. Attested by Tho. S. Sydnor, Gent

299. 1839. Sep 9 -- Examd & found to be correct. Attested by Wm Harding Gent

300. a scar on the right arm occasioned by a burn.

301. 1839. Oct. 14. Examd & found to be correct. Attested by

302. a scar on the lesser toe & top of the right foot.

303. 1839. Oct. 14. Examd & found to be correct. Attested by

304. 1839. Nov. Exd & found to be correct. Attested by Wm Harding Gent

305. 1839. Nov 11. Examd & found correct. Attested by Wm P. Booth Gent

306. 1839. Nov 11. Examd & found correct. Attested by J Deshields Gent

307. North^d County Court 12 Nov. 1839. Exd & found correct. Attested by Ro. Alexander Gent.

308. 1840 Feb 10 Exam^d & found correct. Attested by Wm Harding Gent.

309. 1840 Feb 10 Exam^d & found correct. Attested by Wm Harding Gent.

310. 1840 Feb 10 Exam^d & found correct. Attested by Wm Harding Gent.

311. 1840 Feb 10 Exam^d & found correct. Attested by Wm Harding Gent.

312. 1840 March 9 Examined & found correct. Attested by Robt Alexander gent.

313. 1840 March 10 Examined & found correct. Attested by Wm Harding Gent.

314. 1841 Oct 11 Exd & found correct. Attested by Wm Harding Gent.

315. 1840 April 13 Examined & found to be correct. Attested by Tho. S. Sydnor Gent.

316. 1840 June 8 Examd & found correct. Attested by J. Deshields Gent.

317. 1840 June 8 Examd & found correct. Attested by Wm. Blackwell Gent.

318. 1840 July 13. Exd & found correct. Attested by J. Deshields Gent.

319. 1840 July 13. Exd & found correct. Attested by J. Deshields Gent.

320. 1840 July 13. Exd & found correct. Attested by J. Deshields Gent.

321. Exd 14 Sep 1840 & found correct. Attested by Tho. S. Sydnor, Gent.

322. 1841. Jany 11. Examd & found correct. Attested by R. Alexander Gent.

323. 1841. Jany 11. Exd & found correct. Attested by D Cax Gent.

324. 1841. Jany 11. Exd & found correct. Attested by J. H. Harding Gent.

325. 1841. Mar 9. Exd & found correct. Attested by T. S. Sydnor, Gent.

326. 1841. Mar 8. Exd & found correct. Attested by Wm Harding Gent.

327. 1841. July 12. Exd & found correct. Attested by D. Cox Gent.

328. 11 July 1842. Exd & found correct. Attested by Tho. S. Sydnor Gent.

329. 1842 Apl 11. Exd & found correct. Attested by Wm R. Booth Gent.

330. 1842 Feb 14. Exd & found correct. Attested by Tho. S. Sydnor Gent.

331. 1842 Apl 11. Exd & found correct. Attested by Wm B Booth Gent.

332. 1842 May 9. Exd by the court & found correct. Attested by

333. 11 July 1842. Exd by the court & found correct. Attested by Ro. Alexander Gent.

334. 9 Aug 1842. Exd by the court & found correct. Attested by J. Basye Gent.

335. 1842 Oct° 10. Exd & found correct. Attested by Wm. Harding Gent.

336. 1842 Oct° 10. Exd & found correct. Attested by Wm. Harding Gent.

337. 1842 Nov 15. Exd & found correct. Attested by W. B. Davenport Gent.

338. 1843 Feb 13. Exd & found correct. Attested by Tho S Sydnor, Gent.

339. a scar on the back of the right hand & under lip.

340. 1843 Feb. 13. Exd & found correct. Attested by Tho. S. Sydnor Gent

341. 1843 Feb. 13. Exd & found correct. Attested by Tho. S. Sydnor Gent.

342. 1843 Feb 13. Exd & found correct. Attested by Tho. S Sydnor Gent.

343. A scar over the left eyebrow also on the right thumb.

344. 1843 Feb 13. Exd & found correct. Attested by Wm. Harding Gent.

345. 1843 Feb 13. Exd & found correct. Attested by Tho. S Sydnor Gent.

346. 1843 Feb 13. Exd & found correct. Attested by Tho. S Sydnor Gent.

347. 1843 Feb 13. Exd & found correct.

348. 1843 May 8. Exd & found correct. Attested by Tho. S Sydnor Gent.

349. 1843 May 8. Exd & found correct. Attested by J. M. Smith Gent.

350. 1843 Nov 13 Ex^d & found correct. Attested by Wm Harding Gent.

351. 1843 Nov 13 Ex^d & found correct. Attested by Wm Harding Gent.

352. 1843 Nov 13 Ex^d & found correct. Attested by Wm Harding Gent.

353. 1843 Nov 13 Ex^d & found correct. Attested by Wm Harding Gent.

354. 1843 Nov 13 Ex^d & found correct. Attested by Wm Harding Gent.

355. 1843 Nov 13 Ex^d & found correct. Attested by Wm Harding Gent.

356. 1843 Nov 13 Ex^d & found correct. Attested by Wm Harding Gent.

357. 1843 Nov 13 Ex^d & found correct. Attested by Wm Harding Gent.

358. 1843 Nov 13 Ex^d & found correct. Attested by Wm Harding Gent.

359. 1843 Nov 13 Ex^d & found correct. Attested by Wm Harding Gent.

360. 1843 Nov 13 Ex^d & found correct. Attested by Wm Harding Gent.

361. 1843 Nov 13 Ex^d & found correct. Attested by Wm Harding Gent.

362. 1843 Nov 13 Ex^d & found correct. Attested by Wm Harding Gent.

363. 1844 Jany 8 Ex^d & found correct attested by Js. Haynie Gent.

364. 1845 Sep. 8th Ex^d & found correct attested by C. Harding Gent.

365. 1844 Mar 11. Ex^d & found correct attested by Jos Deshields Gent.

366. 1844 Mar. 12 Ex^d & found correct attested by Tho S. Sydnor Gent.

367. Ex^d 13 May 1844 attested by Tho. S Sydnor Gent.

368. Ex^d 13 May 1844 attested by Tho. S. Sydnor Gent.

369. Ex^d 13 May 1844 attested by Tho. S. Sydnor Gent.

370. Ex^d 14 May 1844 attested by Wm Harding Gent.

371. Exam^d 10 June 1844 found correct attested by J Basye Gent.

372. Manumitted by the will of Cyrus Sutton.

373. Ex^d 8 July 1844 & found correct attested by Tho. S. Sydnor Gent.

374. Attested by Tho. S. Sydnor Gent Ex^d 9th Sep 1844.

375. 1844 Sep 9. Ex^d & found correct attested by

376. 1844 Sep 9. Ex^d & found correct attested by

377. 1844 Nov 11. Ex^d & found correct attested by

378. born of free parents in Essex County.

379. Dec 9th 1844 Exd & found correct.   Robt Alexander.

380. 1845 Feb 10 Exd & found correct attested by Jos. Basye Gent.

381. 1845 Feb 10 Exd & found correct attested by Jos. Basye Gent.

382. 1845 Mar 11 Exd & found correct attested by

383. 1845 June 9th Exd & found correct attested by J. Deshields Gent.

384. 1845 June 9th Exd & found correct attested by J. Deshields Gent.

385. 1845 June 9th Exd & found correct attested by J. Deshields Gent.

386. a burn on the right wrist & a scar on the left temple & upper lip.

387. 1847 March 9th

388. 1847 April 12th.

389. 1847 June 14th.

390. 1847 9th August.

391. 1847 9th August.

392. 23rd August 1847.

393. 14th February 1848.

394. 14th February 1848.

395. 13 February 1848.

396. 13 of August 1849.

397. September 1849.

398. Examined & found to be correct 14 September 1850. Attested by Tho. A. Sydnor JP.

399. Examined by the Court 16 Octobr 1850 -- Attested by JJ Bell.

400. scar on the right cheek near the chin.

401. mark or scar on right side of her neck.

402. Examined by the court & found correct attested by Th^s S. Sydnor.

403. Marks or Scars information in Born Free Column. Born Free information in Marks or Scars column.

404. small scar in the middle of the forehead and right hand drawn with rheumatism.

405. Born in King & Queen County of free parents.

406. marks on right cheek and scar on back of left hand.

407. scar in the right side of his forehead minor near the hair.

408. Examined & found correct 14th October 1850, Attested by Tho. S Sydnor JP.

409. Examined & found correct 14th October 1850, Attested by Tho. S Sydnor JP.

410. Examined & found correct 14th Octr 1850, Attested by Tho. S. Sydnor JP.

411. Burn on left hand & two middle fingers grown together.

412. Burn on inside of left hand and a bone gone out of fore finger in right hand.

413. Examined by the Court & found correct 14th October 1850. Attested by Jno J Betts Jr.

414. Examined by the court 15 October 1850 & found correct. attested by Jno J Bell.

415. Examined by court 14ᵗ Octo 1850 & found correct attested by Jno J. Betts Justice.

416. Examined th 14ᵗ Octobr 1850 by the court & found correct -- attested by Thoˢ S Sydnor.

417. Examined & found correct 14ᵗʰ Octr 1850 -- attested by Tho. S. Sydnor.

418. Examined & found correct 14ᵗʰ Octr 1850 -- attested by Tho. S. Sydnor JP.

419. Examined & found correct 14ᵗʰ Octr 1850 -- attested by Tho. S. Sydnor JP.

420. Examined by the court & found correct 14 Oct. 1850. Attested by Tho S Sydnor.

421. Examined by the court & found correct 14 Oct. 1850. Attested by Thomas S Sydnor.

422. scar across her nose and on left rist.

423. Examined by the court & found correct 14 Oct. 1850. Attested by Tho S Sydnor.

424. scar on left rist and moal on right side of the neck.

425. Examined by the court & found correct 14 Oct. 1850. Attested by

426. Examined by the court & found correct 14 Oct. 1850. Attested by Tho S Sydnor, Jr. (JP).

427. Examined & found correct 14ᵗʰ Octr 1850 Attested Tho S. Sydnor, JP.

428. scar in roots of the hair in left side forehead. small scar in left cheek bone.

429. Examined by the Court & found correct -- attested Thoˢ S. Sydnor 14 October 1850.

430. scar in the roots of her hair on the left side.

431. Examined by the court & found correct 14 October 1850 -- attested Thos S. Sydnor. JP.

432. Examined by the court & found correct 14 October 1850 -- Jno J Bell, Justice.

107

433. Examined by the court & found correct 14 October 1850 -- Attested by Jno J Bell, Justice.

434. Examined by the court & found correct 16 October 1850 -- attested by J J Betts Justice.

435. Examined by the court & found correct 16 October 1850 -- Attested by Thos S Sydnor J P.

436. Examined by the court & found correct 16 October 1850 -- Attested by Thos S Sydnor J P.

437. left eye out & scar on upper part of left arm.

438. Examined by the court & found correct 16 October 1850 -- Attested by Thos S Sydnor J P.

439. Examined by the court & found correct 15 October 1850 -- Attested by Thos S Sydnor J P.

440. Examined by the court & found correct 15 October 1850 -- Attested by Jno. J. Betts Justice.

441. Examined by the court & found correct 11th November 1850 -- attested by Thos S. Sydnor.

442. 28th November 1850: reviewed & attested by Thos S. Sydnor.

443. 11 February 1851 Examined by the court & found correct.

444. 23rd April 1851. Certified by Justice Sydnor assisted by ?

445. small mark on left hand & left cheek.

446. 10 June 1851 certified by

447. Examined by the court & found correct 14th July 1851 attested by Thos S Sydnor.

448. Examined by the court & found correct 11th August 1851. Attested by John J Betts.

449. Examined by the Court & found to be correct 8 September 1851 -- attested by Jno J Betts, a Justice of the Peace.

450. Examined by the Court & found to be correct 8 September 1851 -- attested by Jno J. Betts -- JP.

451. Examined by the Court & found to be correct 8 September 1851.

452. Examined by the Court & found to be correct 8 September 1851.

453. Examined by the Court & found to be correct 8 September 1851.

454. 8 September 1851. Examined by the Court & found to be correct .

455. 8 September 1851. Examined by the Court & found to be correct .

456. 8 September 1851. Examined by the Court & found to be correct.

457. 8 September 1851. Examined by the Court & found to be correct .

458. 8 September 1851. Examined by the Court & found to be correct .

459. 8 September 1851 Examined by the Court & found correct.

460. 13 October 1851. Examined by the Court & found correct on the 12 Decm 1851 Attested by John J. Bell.

461. 13 October 1851. Examined by the Court & found correct .

462. 13 October 1851. Examined by the Court & found correct -- Attested by John J. Betts the 12th December 1851.

463. 13 October 1851. Examined by the Court & found correct -- Attested by John J. Betts the 12th December 1851.

464. 13 October 1851. Examined by the Court & found correct -- Attested by John J. Betts the 12th December 1851.

465. 13 October 1851. Examined by the Court & found correct -- Attested by John J. Betts the 12th December 1851.

466. 13 October 1851. Examined by the Court & found correct -- Attested by John J. Betts the 12th December 1851.

467. 13 October 1851. Examined by the Court & found correct -- Attested by John J. Betts the 12th December 1851.

468. 13 October 1851. Examined by the Court & found correct -- Attested by John J. Betts the 12th December 1851.

469. 10 November 1851. Examined by the Court & found correct -- Attested by John J. Betts the 12th December 1851.

470. 10 November 1851 Examined by the Court and found correct. Attested by Thomas Sydnor ? 1851.

471. Born of Free Parents in Essex County.

472. December 8, 1851 Examined by Court and found Correct. Attested by ? Bell this ? day of December 1851.

473. scar on left side of the neck.

474. July 12th 1852 Examined by Court and found Correct attested by Robert Henderson same day.

475. with a small scar on right cheek.

476. Papers delivered to W. Lee the 16 December 1857.

477. Papers deld to Philip Jackson 15 June 1858.

478. Scar on the right Ear examined by the Court & found to be correct.

BIBLIOGRAPHY

BIBLIOGRAPHY

Bennett, Lerone Jr. *Before the Mayflower: A History of Black America*. Chicago: Johnson Publishing Company, 1962; 6th rev. ed., New York: Penguin Books, 1993.

Berlin, Ira. "From Creole to African: Atlantic Creoles and the Origins of African-American Society in Mainland North America." *The William & Mary Quarterly*. Third Series. LIII (April 1996): pp. 251-288.

Beverley, Robert. *The History and Present State of Virginia*, ed. Louis B. Wright. Chapel Hill: University of North Carolina Press, 1947.

Breen, T. H. and Stephen Innes. *"Myne Owne Ground": Race and Freedom on Virginia's Eastern Shore, 1640-1676*. New York: Oxford University Press, 1980.

Brown, Kathleen Mary. "Gender and the Genesis of a Race and Class System in Virginia, 1630-1750." Ph.D. Diss. The University of Wisconsin - Madison, 1990.

Deal, Douglas. "A Constricted World Free Blacks on Virginia's Eastern Shore, 1680-1750." In *Colonial Chesapeake Society*, ed. Lois Green Carr, Philip D. Morgan, and Jean B. Russo, pp. 275-305. Chapel Hill: The University of North Carolina Press, 1988.

Department of Commerce and Labor. Bureau of the Census. S. N. D. North, Director. *Heads of Families at the First Census of the United States taken in the Year 1790. Records of the State Enumerations: 1782 to 1785 -- Virginia*. Washington: Government Printing Office, 1908.

Doggett, Barbara Lynn. "Parish Apprenticeship in Colonial Virginia. A Study of Northumberland County, 1680-1695 and 1750-1765." M.A. Thesis, College of William and Mary, 1981.

"Genealogist, James D. Walker, Dies at Age 65." *The Washington Post* 8 October 1993.

Guild, June Purcel, LLM. *Black Laws of Virginia: A Summary of the Legislative Acts of Virginia concerning Negroes from Earliest Times to the Present*. Whettet & Shepperson, 1936; reprint, New York: Negro Universities Press, 1969.

Morgan, Philip D. "Slave Life in Piedmont Virginia, 1720-1800." In *Colonial Chesapeake Society*, ed. Lois Green Carr, Philip D. Morgan, and Jean B. Russo, pp. 433-484. Chapel Hill: The University of North Carolina Press, 1988.

Norris, Walter Biscoe R., ed. *Westmoreland County, Virginia: 1653-1983.* Montross, VA: Westmoreland County Board of Supervisors, 1983.

Quarles, Benjamin. "The Colonial Militia and Negro Manpower." *The Mississippi Valley Historical Review.* XLV (March 1959): pp. 644-645.

Thorndale, William. "The Virginia Census of 1619," *Magazine of Virginia Genealogy* 33 (Summer 1995): pp. 156-170.

Wheeler, Robert Anthony. "Lancaster County, Virginia, 1650-1750: The Evolution of a Southern Tidewater Community." Ph.D. Diss., Brown University, 1972.

Wood, Peter H. "I Did the Best I Could Do for My Day: The Study of Early Black History During the Second Reconstruction, 1960 to 1976." *The William and Mary Quarterly* 35 (April 1976): pp. 185-225.

Woodson, Carter G. *Free Negro Heads of Families in the United States in 1830 together with a Brief Treatment of the Free Negro.* Washington: The Association for the Study of Negro Life and History, Inc., 1923.

Workers of the Writers' Program of the Works Projects Administration in the State of Virginia, comp. *The Negro in Virginia.* New York: Hastings House, 1940; reprint Winston-Salem: John F. Blair, Publisher, 1994.

INDEX

INDEX

Bell
Ann . . . 35
Coleman . . . 35, 55
Dorcas Kelly . . . 35
Elizabeth . . . 51
James . . . 39
Jane . . . 49, 56
JJ . . . 67
Jno J . . . 71, 74
John . . . 33, 36, 47
John J. . . . 79
Mary . . . 35, 47
Sally . . . 49, 56
William . . . 80

Berlin
Dr. Ira . . . 1

Betts
John J. . . . 79
John S. . . . 77
Thomas D. . . . 80

Betty . . . 32

Bird
James . . . 54

Black . . . 13
African disenfranchisement . . . 2
meaning of word . . . 3
Robt. . . . 13, 18

black (color) 14, 15, 33, 34, 37, 39, 55-57, 59, 61, 73

black (mark) . . . 19, 22-24, 31

Black Laws . . . 6

blacks
control of . . . 6
first . . . 2
Free . . . vii, 3, 6, 18

blacks
nonslave . . . 2, 6

Blackwell
J. . . . 38
Wm. . . . 51

Blueford
Wm. . . . 57

Blundon
Alice . . . 54, 77
James . . . 65
John . . . 14, 19, 75
Rufus . . . 77
Samuel . . . 75
Sarah Ann . . . 75
Virginia . . . 75

Boid
Austin . . . 43

Born Free 11, 14, 24, 30-34, 36, 37, 46, 57, 67

Born Free of a White Mother . . . 14

Boyd
Baldwin . . . 60
Eliza . . . 61, 66
James . . . 14
Lucy . . . 34
Thomas . . . 55
Wm. . . . 15

Bradger
Elizabeth . . . 64

Brenn
Lilly . . . 38
Sally . . . 38

Burk
Ellen . . . 31

Burke
Ellen . . . 44

Campbell
Eliza . . . 15

Caroline County
Born of free parents in . . . 37

Carpenter
Alexander . . . 75
Ben . . . 59
Benja . . . 31
Bertha . . . 56
Betsy . . . 42, 47, 77
Carlos . . . 43
Eliz. . . . 59
Elizabeth . . . 66
Elizabeth Francis . . . 72
Griffin . . . 33, 40, 47
Hiram . . . 48, 59, 65
Jas. . . . 39
Mary . . . 30, 48
Mary Jane . . . 72
May . . . 65
Molly . . . 30, 38, 47
Nancy . . . 30, 43
Robert . . . 30, 43
Rufus Henry . . . 73
Spencer . . . 23
Tho. . . . 42
Whittington . . . 23

Carter
Robert . . . 23
Robt. . . . 34

Casity
Elizabeth . . . 66, 74
Emeline . . . 73

124

scar